BAUDELAIRE'S *Voyages*

The Poet and His Painters

Jeffrey Coven
with an essay by Dore Ashton

An Exhibition Organized by The Heckscher Museum

A Bulfinch Press Book
Little, Brown and Company
Boston · New York · Toronto · London

First Edition

Library of Congress Cataloging-in-Publication Data
Coven, Jeffrey.
        Baudelaire's voyages: the poet and his painters / Jeffrey
        Coven; with an essay by Dore Ashton.
                p.   cm.
        "An exhibition organized by the Heckscher Museum."
        Includes index.
                        ISBN 0-8212-1999-5
        1. Baudelaire, Charles, 1821–1867—Knowledge—Art—
        Exhibitions.   2. Art and literature—France—History—
        19th century—Exhibitions.   3. Baudelaire, Charles,
        1821–1867—Illustrations—Exhibitions.   4. French
        poetry—Illustrations—Exhibitions.   I. Ashton, Dore.
        II. Heckscher Museum.   III. Title.
                        PQ2191.Z5C65   1993
841'.8—dc20   93-19922

Bulfinch Press is an imprint and trademark of Little, Brown
and Company (Inc.)

Published simultaneously in Canada by Little, Brown
& Company (Canada) Limited

PRINTED IN ITALY

This book has been published in conjunction with the
exhibition *Baudelaire's Voyages: The Poet and His Painters,*
organized by Jeffrey Coven, Guest Curator, Heckscher
Museum:
    Heckscher Museum, Huntington, New York,
    August 28–November 14, 1993
    Archer M. Huntington Gallery, University of Texas
    at Austin, January 21–March 13, 1994

This project is made possible by a generous grant from the
Florence Gould Foundation and by general operating support
provided by the Institute of Museum Services, a federal
agency, the New York State Council on the Arts, a state
agency, and the Town of Huntington.

Permission to reproduce works of art has been granted by
the lenders except where noted otherwise.

FRONTISPIECE:
Gustave Courbet, *Portrait of Baudelaire,* 1847

Courbet's portrait of Baudelaire reading was done during the
period of the Revolution of 1848, when the two men were
close friends and political allies and before their relationship
cooled over Baudelaire's criticism of Courbet's realism as a
"war against the imagination." The portrait is strikingly similar
to the image of Baudelaire that appears in *The Painter's Studio*
(FIG. 16).

Contents

This book is in memory of my mother, Trudy,
and my father, Ben, and for my brother, Larry.

Preface and Acknowledgments

Recently I mentioned to a colleague that I was writing a book about Charles Baudelaire. "Ah, Baudelaire," he said, and his eyes lit up with a knowing leer. Certainly my colleague is not alone in his impression of this poet whose attachment to the power of the sensual has stirred up the interest of generations of readers, including those representatives of the French state who prosecuted and convicted him in 1857 for obscenity and banned several of the poems in *Les Fleurs du mal*. More assiduous readers of Baudelaire's book, however, cannot escape what he called its "terrible morality" and his purpose, which was to express his loathing of sin and vice, his compassion for suffering mankind, and the sources of his "anger and melancholy."

Also attracted to the more titillating qualities of his poetry have been generations of illustrators who, bent on further enticing those readers for whom Baudelaire is synonymous with prurience, have spiced up edition after edition of *Les Fleurs du mal* with drawings ranging from the erotic to the frankly pornographic, revealing, as John Russell has noted, "more about the illustrator [or perhaps the publisher] than about the great lord of language who wrote the poems." This present study of visual art related to Baudelaire's poetry does not concern itself with that body of work. Rather, it seeks to reveal the powerful correspondences (the word Baudelaire chose to describe the interconnectedness of the arts) between the work of some of the Western world's greatest artists and Baudelaire's poetry, with its themes of the irreparable attachment to sin, the inextricable combination of glamour and suffering threaded into the fabric of life in the modern city, and the ultimately futile but nevertheless uplifting quest of the artist seeking to escape suffering through art. Most of what this book has to offer will come from appreciating such correspondences. The heart of the matter lies in experiencing the poetry and the pictures together, and it is my hope that readers will focus their attention on that. I have tried through my commentaries to add to the richness of that experience.

It should be noted that this is not a comprehensive presentation of the relationships between Baudelaire's poetry and visual art. Anyone familiar with this subject will recognize that the material here is selective and that a number of documented relationships between specific Baudelaire poems and various works of art have not been illustrated or discussed. The selection comprises artists and their works that represent some characteristic relationships between visual art and Baudelaire's poetry as well as some idiosyncratic ones. It includes works by artists who came before Baudelaire and inspired him, by those who were his contemporaries and friends and with whom he shared concerns, and by those who came after him and were influenced by his poetry.

Special emphasis has been given to poem-picture relationships included in *Baudelaire's Voyages,* the exhibition organized by me for the Heckscher Museum and for which this volume serves as a companion and catalogue. The exhibition is organized on the basis of groups of visual images related to specific poems. For example, in the exhibition the text of the poem "L'Irréparable" is accompanied by works of Rodin, Manet, Grasset, Daumier, Degas, Lautrec, and Rouault, each of which corresponds to a particular passage in the poem. Baudelaire's mind, a storehouse of images garnered from his life as an art critic and lover of art, often yielded poems that bore relationships with the work of a number of different artists. The book incorporates a similar motif but also affords the possibility of exploring those relationships in greater depth by including some poems and artworks that were not available for exhibition. For a complete listing of works that appeared in the exhibition, see the checklist on pages 173–176. Readers who wish to explore still further connections between Baudelaire's poetry and art are referred to the bibliography.

Baudelaire's poetry is divided into two general categories, his verse poems, which are generally collected under the title of *Les Fleurs du mal (The Flowers of Evil),* and his prose poems, volumes of which have appeared under several titles. The most common are *Petits poèmes en prose (Little Prose Poems)* and *Le Spleen de Paris (Paris Spleen).* I have chosen to refer to them collectively by the latter title because it combines two elements — Paris and spleen — close to the author's heart. The poems included in *Baudelaire's Voyages* represent, of course, only a small portion of Baudelaire's poetic œuvre and have been selected because of their relevance to various works of visual art. Because of space limitations, passages rather than entire poems are sometimes reproduced.

Poems and passages are presented in the original French followed by a translation in English prose. (The prose has been divided into lines approximately equivalent to the verse lines in order to make the translations easier to follow.) Prose has been used for two reasons. First, translations of poetry, no matter how fine, are never an adequate substitute for the original. Second, translators of poetry have many concerns other than imagery. In an attempt to incorporate meter, rhyme, and other poetic elements, correspondences with visual art that appear in the original may be obscured. In the prose translations, I have tried to maintain the bases for those correspondences. In most cases I have attempted to make the translations as literal as possible, though on occasion, in order that they not stray too far from English syntax or other English-language conventions, I have made what I hope are judicious adjustments. My goal has been to communicate Baudelaire's content, especially where it relates to a picture, without completely abandoning his poetic intent as far as I understand it. If these translations are serviceable in this regard, they will have fulfilled my limited purpose. For whatever violations of the originals are present, and there inevitably will be many, I take full responsibility.

Quotations from Baudelaire other than poetry (letters, criticism, etc.) are given in English translation only, except in a few cases where the French seemed especially important or enriching. The translators are specified in the notes.

My sources for the relationships between Baudelaire's poetry and works of visual art are preeminently the scholars and other commentators who over a long period of time and through careful work have made note of them. Much of what I have done here has been to assemble the associations they have made. To their work I have added some of my own impressions based on my study of his poetry and my searches through the works of artists who seemed to me to have a kinship with the poet.

Among those whose work was indispensable for this book are Jean Prévost, Jean Pommier, Claude Pichois, Georges Poulet, Lois Boe Hyslop, Francis E. Hyslop, F. W. Leakey, and Richard D.E. Burton. There are of course many others, including those who have written about the artists and in the process delineated relationships with the poet. They are all cited in the notes and the bibliography. For much of the value that is here, I am indebted to them.

The exhibition *Baudelaire's Voyages: The Poet and His Painters* has four parts: "Voyage into the Depths," "Voyage into the City," "Voyage into the Dream," and "Voyage into the New" each reflecting a major motif in Baudelaire's art. The book contains a chapter for each of these "voyages" except the last, which is treated by me only in a coda at the conclusion of "Voyage into the Dream." Dore Ashton's essay, "Baudelaire, Irremediable Modern," which begins the book, serves, however, to remedy this omission far better than I could have done and does much more as well.

For a project such as this, which includes the exhibition as well as the book, thanks are due to many. First, I would like to express my gratitude to the Heckscher Museum and especially its curator (and the project director for *Baudelaire's Voyages*), Anna C. Noll, whose expertise and support were crucial to all aspects of the exhibition and the book. The enormous amount of work she did — always first-rate — is itself deserving of special commendation. It also was she who first interested Bulfinch Press in the project, and it was her experience and vigilance that helped me avoid so many of the pitfalls into which a novice in the curatorial world would otherwise certainly have stumbled.

Also at the Heckscher thanks go to Director John E. Coraor, the Board of Trustees, Education Coordinator Melissa Erb, and especially the Registrar, William H. Titus, whose competence, good humor, and thorough professionalism were always evident and appreciated. Curators and other individuals associated with various museums and collections or members of the art community who were helpful, informative and even kindly were numerous. I cannot mention them all but among them were Ethel Baziotes, Ellen Hirschland, Jay McKean Fisher of the Baltimore Museum of Art, Wendy Weitman of the Museum of Modern Art,

Colta Ives and Suzanne Boorsch of the Metropolitan Museum of Art, Christine Wachter of the Blum Helman Gallery, Joan Banach of the Dedalus Foundation, George Shackelford of the Houston Museum of Fine Arts, Meg Graselli, Lisa Mariam, and Gregory Jecmen of the National Gallery of Art, Robert Rainwater of the New York Public Library, and most especially Roberta Waddell, Curator of Prints at the New York Public Library, and her staff members Margaret Glover and Nancy Finlay, whose consistent support and patience were invaluable and downright indispensable.

Without the sabbatical leave granted to me to work on this project by Suffolk Community College, it could not have been completed, and my colleagues there who helped in various ways include Professors Giuseppe Battista, Michael Gerien, Barbara Karyo, Zina Mazura, and Liliane Thurau. For reading early versions of the manuscript and even more for their warm feelings and support, I would like to thank my friends Alice Elman, Richard Elman, and Ivan Sanders. The support of the Frank R. Melville Jr. Library at the State University of New York at Stony Brook was also indispensable, and I especially appreciated the cooperation of the Director of Circulation, Janet Cavanagh, and the Curator of Special Collections, Evert Volkersz. Thanks also to Brenda Coven for her skill as a bibliographic researcher as well as her sensitive and intelligent advice. To Dore Ashton extraordinary appreciation is no less due for her kindness and support than for her consistently wise suggestions. Her confidence in me and the project was always present and counted for more than she probably knows. It was her notion that started us all off toward making the catalogue into a book, and it was she who introduced me to Caroline Press, whose services as my agent and critical reader proved consistently thorough and valuable.

To Bulfinch Press I want to express my thanks in general for the high editorial standards they maintain in a world where such concerns seem to be fading away, and specifically to Brian Hotchkiss for seeing enough value in this project to recommend it for publication and for his patience with me throughout. Martine Bruel, the designer of the book, has added immeasurable beauty and value to it. Dorothy Williams, Associate Editor, and Betsy Pitha, Senior Copy Editor, were nothing short of invaluable. Their astute and sensitive suggestions and the improvements resulting from them permeate the book. For her careful and extraordinarily intelligent editing of the manuscript, I am more than grateful to Debra Edelstein.

Without friends, few would want to undertake anything. My thanks to those who were around when needed and understanding when I was not, particularly Lois Ambash, Gary Goodwin, and Steven Klipstein.

And I could not have managed any of this without Leslie Brett, who through her steadfastness and caring found all those volumes on Baudelaire and his artists in the dustiest corners of bookshops, produced the bibliography for this volume, and, in general, kept me going.

Finally, I pay homage to Baudelaire, whose mind and art afforded me the pleasure and the privilege of working on this project.

For whatever shortcomings are here, the ones I already know about and the many others that will be discovered, I take full credit myself.

J.C.

Note: All quotations in French from Baudelaire's works are from *Œuvres complètes,* ed. Claude Pichois (2 vols.; Paris: Gallimard, Bibliothèque de la Pléiade, 1975–76). When a quotation is not identified by title in the text, the volume and page numbers in this edition are given in parentheses.

Except where otherwise specified, English translations of Baudelaire's critical prose are from Charles Baudelaire, *The Painter of Modern Life and Other Essays,* ed. and trans. Jonathan Mayne (London: Phaidon, 1964); and Charles Baudelaire, *Art in Paris 1845–1862,* ed. and trans. Jonathan Mayne (London: Phaidon, 1965). These volumes are cited in the notes as Mayne, *Painter,* and Mayne, *Art.*

Unattributed translations of Baudelaire's critical prose and correspondence and all translations of Baudelaire's poems are by the authors of this book.

The exhibition and book *Baudelaire's Voyages: The Poet and His Painters* has been a singular accomplishment for the Heckscher Museum. It is the Museum's initial copublishing venture, and for the first time in decades all the Museum's galleries have been turned over to a single exhibition.

There are many people to thank for their involvement in an event of such magnitude. First and foremost, we wish to thank Jeffrey Coven for approaching the Heckscher Museum with his idea of an exhibition on the relationship between visual art and the poetry of Charles Baudelaire. It was a pleasure to watch Professor Coven's ideas grow, take shape, and refine themselves over the past two and a half years. His devotion to his subject was exemplary and the amount of work he accomplished formidable, especially in light of his teaching duties and the short lead time for the project. The Heckscher Museum is also grateful to Dore Ashton for her contributions as a guest essayist and curatorial consultant and for her wise suggestion that we pursue a copublisher for the book.

I am especially thankful for the opportunity to work with Brian Hotchkiss, Senior Editor at Bulfinch Press, who saw the worth in *Baudelaire's Voyages* and took a chance on a small museum with no commercial publishing experience. Without his and his staff's unflagging support this publication would not have been possible. Also to be thanked is Robin Straus, the Museum's literary agent, who cheerfully and diligently guided us through the contract negotiations.

The support of Jonathan Bober, Curator of Prints and Drawings at the Archer M. Huntington Gallery at the University of Texas at Austin, has been invaluable. Because of his interest in the project at its very early stages, we were able to share the exhibition with his institution and thereby reach a much wider audience.

Partial funding for the exhibition and catalogue has been provided by a major grant from the Florence Gould Foundation. We are deeply indebted to them for their generosity, particularly in light of the many high-quality proposals which they can choose among to support.

Our sincere appreciation is extended to the museums, libraries, galleries, private foundations, and individuals who have so graciously agreed to lend many important works of art to *Baudelaire's Voyages*. Without their cooperation the exhibition would not have been possible. I would also like to thank the many colleagues and friends who offered support, advice, and a sense of humor to me during the long and detailed process of overseeing this project. In particular, I wish to express my gratitude to Sharon Blume, Peggy Cleary, John Taormina, and Salli and Jerome Zimmerman, who were always there with a sympathetic ear.

Anna C. Noll
Project Director

2 Paul Cézanne, *Three Skulls,* 1902–1906

Baudelaire, Irremediable Modern

by Dore Ashton

A hidden spring, tapped now and then by those with the diviner's instinct. Now the poetry, now the prose. For certain temperaments, a presence in perpetuity. Baudelaire — a man of his time, but also a man whose time, like those metaphorical clocks he so often named (like, in fact, Cézanne's implacable black clock), was modern, which is to say, our uneasy familiar. In Baudelaire's work "the ephemeral, the fugitive, the contingent, the half of art whose other half is the eternal and immutable"[1] arrive in an unstable mélange that reminds us of our own irremediable modernity, as he defined it. His words speak intermittently to generation after generation, and especially to artists.

Baudelaire endeared himself to artists first by means of his rapt and intelligent attention and then in his repeated avowals of the importance to him of painted images. In his *Journaux intimes (Intimate Journals)* he noted a task to be undertaken: "To glorify the cult of pictures, my great, my unique, my primitive passion."[2] He confessed, in his "Salon de 1859," that "even in my extreme youth my eyes had never been able to drink their fill of painted or sculptured images, and I think that worlds could have come to an end, *impavidum ferient,* before I had become an iconoclast."[3] Such a poet could not help but engage the interest of artists — the many with whom he consorted in his lifetime and the many who have heard him since. In his poetry artists find great tributes to their own imagery (poems that draw upon subjects as imagined by artists, such as the labyrinthine stairways of Piranesi or the lonely fall of Icarus by Bruegel). In his prose they find perdurable insights, such as his comment that Daumier "drew because he had the need to draw — ineluctable vocation," or that Goya was a modern in his "love of the ungraspable" and his "feeling for violent contrasts," or that Delacroix's color "thinks for itself, independent of the objects it clothes."[4] In addition, Baudelaire's definition of modernity, inhabiting poems and prose alike, meets the needs of certain temperaments that, like Baudelaire's own, cannot accept the confinement of the merely quotidian. They find in him sudden and rare intuitions — shocks, as he sometimes called them — that illuminate their own struggle. There is consolation in that. Perhaps, above all, artists find the candid, searingly candid, record of a deep and exacting experience as creator and as profoundly sensitive receptor of the created. There are painters still today who find in him a *semblable,* a *frère.*

Baudelaire's passion for images impelled him into artistic circles in his early youth, when he commenced his lifelong inquiry into the ways of artists. He well knew the smell of the studio, the tools of the painter, the idiosyncratic working procedures. He engaged in discussions and learned the secret language of shoptalk. He asked questions. He listened. Above all, listened. Instinctively he sought the historical dimensions of each arresting image and, as a good critic, moved from a work on the easel back to its emotional antecedents and forward to its potential opening out — its modernity. A word he liked and used both in prose and poetry was "concatenation." It is remarkable how, as an art critic, he discerned the concatenations that would eventually reveal the biography of what we today call modern art. To begin with, he spied out Goya as a precursor. Goya, one of Baudelaire's beacons, "cauchemar plein de choses inconnues" (1:13; "nightmare filled with unknown things"), was essential in the chain that eventually linked Goya to Manet and

Manet to Picasso. Manet, with whom Baudelaire spent so many important afternoons, had so much admired Goya's two *majas* that he asked the photographer Nadar to make enlarged photographs for him. And Baudelaire, during his last illness, chose for the wall of his hospital room a painting by Manet and a copy of Goya's portrait of the Duchess of Alba.

Baudelaire recognized Goya not only for his love of the ungraspable but also for his volatile modernity skidding on the edge of the abyss. "It may very well be that Goya intended to suggest, a good forty years before Baudelaire, the demonic, the monstrous nature of bare sensuality robbed of ulterior meanings," wrote Fred Licht about the *majas*. "Goya in this oblique fashion is the first painter to make us aware of the disturbingly equivocal qualities of love in the secularized world." Licht also identified the modern's strange reversion to the medieval sin of acedia, that state of spiritual sloth — a tendency Baudelaire lamented in himself. Goya, Licht finds, offers "a clear foretaste of Poe's paralyzing intuitions of nothingness and of Baudelaire's spleen and ennui. The demon of acedia steals all the luster from the world's sunlight, jeers at our comings and goings, and mocks all pretensions."[5] T. S. Eliot, that clarion of modernism, whose work, despite his reflexive distaste for Baudelaire, was deeply affected by his example, also identifies Baudelaire's ennui as "a true form of *acedia,* arising from the unsuccessful struggle toward the spiritual life":

> It is not merely in the use of imagery of common life, not merely in the use of imagery of the sordid life of the metropolis, but in the elevation of such imagery to the *first intensity* — presenting it as it is, and yet making it represent something much more than itself — that Baudelaire has created a mode of release and expression for other men.[6]

Eliot comes still closer to his own link with Baudelaire when he says, according to Marianne Moore, that he learned from Baudelaire "of the possibility of fusion between the sordidly realistic and the phantasmagoric, the possibility of the juxtaposition of the matter-of-fact and the fantastic."[7]

In the concatenation of the lines of modern art, after Goya comes Delacroix, who, of all the nineteenth-century painters, provides an indispensable link. He was revered by Cézanne, who in turn was revered by Matisse and Picasso, not the least for his reverence for Delacroix. Baudelaire's peerless art criticism contributed immeasurably to modern art — a rare event, surely — when he heard Delacroix's thoughts and heightened the master's verbal insights, commingling them with his own, to fashion the portrait of the modern artist. This was, of course, a self-portrait. Some of Baudelaire's finest prose writing occurs in his various reviews of Delacroix's accomplishments. Passion, which he insisted a critic must have, was Delacroix's forte. The painter, he said, was "passionately in love with passion."[8] From his first acquaintance with the older artist, Baudelaire experienced a surge of passionate interest that never diminished. He accepted certain key principles to fuse with his own aesthetic discoveries. These he constantly refined and elaborated in poems, letters, and notes. Delacroix's brief observation that "nature is only a dictionary" set Baudelaire off on many pursuits. He was a lover of dictionaries, but he knew that "no one has ever thought of his dictionary as a *composition* in the poetic sense of the word."[9] The poetic sense of the word required that an artist select his hieroglyphs, his analogies, to illuminate the whole of the composition since, as he remarked as early as the "Salon de 1846," "art is nothing but an abstraction and a sacrifice of the detail to the whole."[10]

Baudelaire's idea of abstraction was directly informed by Delacroix's studio talk. From the painter he took the notion of the way to look at a picture: one looks for melody. The right way to know if a picture is melodious, he said in the "Salon de 1846," "is to look at it from far enough away to make it impossible to understand its subject or to distinguish its lines. If it is melodious, it already has a meaning and has already taken its place in your store of memories."[11] This fundamental idea in the history of modern art would reappear, as when Jean-Paul Sartre succinctly remarked that the Mona Lisa didn't *mean* anything, but that it had meaning. Baudelaire elaborated in 1863:

> A well-drawn figure fills you with a pleasure which is absolutely divorced from its subject. Whether voluptuous or awe-inspiring, this figure will owe its entire charm to the arabesque which it cuts in space. So long as it is skillfully drawn, there is nothing — from the limbs of a martyr who is being flayed alive, to the body of a swooning nymph — that does not admit a kind of pleasure in whose elements the subject matter plays no part.[12]

Since Baudelaire's adaptations of Delacroix's thoughts were shaped in memorable prose, their memory lingered in the thoughts of many modern artists. Matisse above all — one of the best stylists among painters who wrote — remembered. Many phrases in his "Notes of a Painter" are almost paraphrases:

> A work of art must carry in itself its complete significance and impose it upon the beholder even before he can identify the subject matter.

Or:

> The whole arrangement of my picture is expressive. The place occupied by figures or objects, the empty spaces around them, the proportions, everything plays a part.

Or:

> I cannot copy nature in a servile way; I must interpret nature and submit it to the spirit of the picture.[13]

It was, after all, Baudelaire's immense effort to get a grasp on the *spirit* of Delacroix's œuvre that tempered all his criticism and filtered into all subsequent art criticism. After Baudelaire, art criticism could no longer pursue its dilatory, cataloguing ways. Baudelaire floated thoughts and suggestions that would grow rather than diminish. It was he who insisted on the idea — certainly, again, from Delacroix — of the arabesque: that figure in mental space that became for the Symbolists a talisman, and that has sinuously wound its way in painting throughout modern art right up to Pollock. In his *Journaux intimes,* Baudelaire twice declared the arabesque the most spiritual, the most ideal of designs, and Matisse on many occasions referred to "his" arabesque, an abstraction weighty with implications. Both Matisse and Picasso, admirers of Delacroix, kept the word "arabesque" in their pictorial vocabularies. Undoubtedly they were interested to discover in Delacroix's journals, a handbook for all modern artists, that the painter had been reading Baudelaire's essays on Edgar Allan Poe and had copied out Poe's citation of Francis Bacon in *Ligeia:* "There is no exquisite beauty without some *strangeness* in the proportion." Such strangeness in proportion became the prime characteristic of their modern draftsmanship.

As divergent as they were in temperament and style, Matisse and Picasso stand as keystones, or, as Kandinsky called them, signposts, in the structure of modern art. Both named as their "father" Cézanne. Deeply woven into Cézanne's approach to his métier were the memories of youthful readings, among which Baudelaire's poetry and criticism were tenaciously retained. There are many testimonies to his devotion to Baudelaire's theories of painting both in Cézanne's letters and, obliquely, in his paintings. Perhaps the most telling evidence was gathered at the end of his life when Cézanne was rereading Baudelaire's poetry. Picasso remarked that "what forces our interest is Cézanne's anxiety — that's Cézanne's lesson."[14] Anxiety, faithful companion of most moderns and one of the compelling motifs in Baudelaire's work, had accompanied Cézanne from his early youth. But in his old age he had transformed it into the pervasive melancholy Baudelaire had painted in so many subtle tones throughout *Les Fleurs du mal,* which Cézanne instantly recognized.

One of the most convincing testimonies of Cézanne's profound engagement with Baudelaire was offered by Léo Larguier, a twenty-three-year-old conscript billeted near Aix who became a welcome visitor to the old painter's studio during 1901–1902. As a sign of friendship, Cézanne gave Larguier his personal copy of *Les Fleurs du mal,* a book whose cover was "bespattered with paint, with touches of red and brown, and perhaps the imprint of a finger that had leaned against the palette."[15] The most precious sign of Cézanne's intimacy with the book — the "ordinary edition" of 1898 — was a list of penciled roman numerals on the last page indicating the poems Cézanne most often reread. Each of the eight poems Cézanne designated offers tantalizing suggestions of his *état d'âme* and could be endlessly excavated (to use one of Baudelaire's favorite and most ambiguous words, as when he says in "Fusées" ["Flares"], "Music excavates the skies"). There are images that, in their poetic — that is, verbal — beauty, must certainly have moved Cézanne. But more important, there are images in which he could find himself, a modern self filled with conflicts and artistic agonies.

The first poem he lists, "Les Phares" ("Beacons"), is, naturally, about painters; it is Baudelaire's tribute to the great chain of art history, to the masters who were "le meilleur témoignage . . . de notre dignité" ("the best evidence . . . of our dignity"). The dark areas of Cézanne's personality, so turbulent, so prey to extreme emotions, responded to Baudelaire's description of Rubens's painted place where "la vie afflue et s'agite sans

cesse, / Comme l'air dans le ciel et la mer dans la mer" ("life seethes and surges endlessly like air in heaven, sea within sea"). The air in the sky he knew and painted. The sea within the sea was certainly a description of his inner state.

The second poem on his list, "Don Juan aux enfers" ("Don Juan in Hell"), about the aged "impenitent," as Richard Howard called him, confirmed Cézanne in his own stubbornness — he who withdrew from society to the fastness of his studio and, like Baudelaire's Don Juan, refused to attend to the reproachful others, but stood, leaning on his sword (his brush), staring at the wake of his ship, and "ne daignait rien voir" ("didn't deign to see anything else").

Cézanne's fifth poem, "Une Charogne" ("A Carrion"), had a special importance. While still in his twenties he had sketched illustrations for it, and in his last years sometimes recited it, entire, to young admirers. One of Baudelaire's most searing and violent poems, it reflected his determination to be totally candid, as he said a modern poet must be; to face the fateful decay of human life that, like the teeming world of flies and larvae in the dead horse's belly, "rendait une étrange musique, / Comme l'eau courante et le vent" ("gave out a strange music like flowing water and wind"). Baudelaire cruelly reminds his mistress that she, too, will end in putrid decay. In his last lines, however, he defies destiny, and in a tribute to the work of art declares: "j'ai gardé la forme et l'essence divine / De mes amours décomposés!" ("I have kept the form and divine essence of my decomposed loves!"). Interestingly, Rodin, almost exactly Cézanne's contemporary and, like Cézanne, considered a "father" of modern art, responded equally strongly to "Une Charogne," and is quoted as having said:

> Let Baudelaire describe festering corpses, unclean, viscid, eaten by worms, and let him but imagine his beloved mistress under this frightful aspect, and

nothing can equal in splendor his picture of this terrible juxtaposition of beauty which we would wish eternal and the atrocious disintegration which awaits it.[16]

On Cézanne's list, the last two poems, "Le Mort joyeux" ("Joyful Death") and "Le Goût du néant" ("Taste for Oblivion"), reveal naked despair and the dark vision that visited him, "ce vieux corps sans âme" ("this old body without a soul") and this "Vieux cheval dont le pied à chaque obstacle bute" ("Old horse who stumbles with each step"). The old marauder, Baudelaire says, has lost his taste for love and even for dispute, and moment by moment time engulfs him. The taste for oblivion, the temptation of the abyss, the alluring mystery of Nothingness, form one of Baudelaire's most distinctive messages for future artists, and it would be explored by a long line of moderns, beginning with his greatest disciple, Arthur Rimbaud, and then Stéphane Mallarmé,

Paul Valéry, Rainer Maria Rilke, Jean-Paul Sartre, and countless painters after the Second World War. They looked into Baudelaire's dark mirror and saw, as did Cézanne, themselves.

Baudelaire's poetic words clearly resounded in the hermetic vessel of Cézanne's memory. His prose words were important in a different way. Despite his disdain for art talk and talkers, Cézanne regularly rummaged in books and journals seeking confirmation of his intuitions concerning art. In 1906, shortly before his death, he wrote to his son that he was rereading *L'Art romantique,* and that Baudelaire was "one of the strong."[17] In the edition he owned, Cézanne could read in "Le Peintre de la vie moderne" ("The Painter of Modern Life") Baudelaire's essay on Constantin Guys, who, though acknowledged as a minor artist, served as a pretext for Baudelaire to work out some of his most eccentric theories. It was in this essay that Baudelaire aired his views on the character of an artist's modernity and warned that the artist who neglects the transitory and fugitive runs the risk of hurtling into the "abyss of an abstract and indeterminate beauty" (2:695). He defines beauty as "always, inevitably of a double composition," qualifying his definition by saying that through the particular temperament of an artist his age will be reflected. Art, he insisted, always reflects a duality that is a "fatal consequence of the duality of man" (2:685). Baudelaire sometimes cloaked his ideal artist in the figure of the dandy, most fully explored in this essay, whose significant characteristic is his "quality of opposition and revolt." Dandies, he wrote, "are all representatives of what is finest in human pride, of that compelling need, alas only too rare today, of combating and destroying triviality" (2:711). The aged Cézanne certainly assented; he insisted on the importance of the motif and yet sought without surcease a transcendental ideal.

But perhaps it was Baudelaire's 1863 tribute to Delacroix that most bestirred him. There Baudelaire gathered many of his own intuitive earlier judgments, and certain views of others, in a challenging critical essay in which he addressed himself to some of the most intimate problems Cézanne confronted. In his final tribute, Baudelaire included passages from his own "Salon de 1859," in which Cézanne's convictions were anticipated. Cézanne dreamed of a fusion, a seamless harmony, especially in his last decade. Baudelaire wrote:

> all the figures, their relative disposition, the landscape or interior which provides them with horizon or background, their garments — everything, in fact, must serve to illuminate the general idea, must wear its original color, its livery, so to speak.[18]

For Cézanne, who sat day in, day out, before the same landscape, seeking to condense and weave each detail into an ideal vision of a harmonious universe, Baudelaire's fundamental formula, expressed most firmly in this essay, answered and consoled him:

> The whole visible universe is but a storehouse of images and signs to which the imagination will give a relative place and a value; it is a sort of pasture which the imagination must digest and transform.[19]

In Cézanne's reading of L'Art romantique, he would encounter the fragments Baudelaire had gathered for an essay, "L'Art philosophique." Judging from Cézanne's late letters and remarks he made to his young admirers during the last decade of his life, Baudelaire's opening paragraph provided a perfect fit to his own ideas:

> What is pure art according to the modern idea? It is the creation of an evocative magic, containing at once the object and the subject, the world external to the artist and the artist himself.[20]

This leading idea, expressed variously in Baudelaire's critical writings, was to be honored by the major founders of modern art and reconsidered throughout the twentieth century.

If the modern artist has a tragic flaw, according to Baudelaire, it is his endemic sense of irony, which, like many of Baudelaire's words, is presented more with boundless suggestiveness than with specificity. "I am the true representative of irony, and my malady is of an absolutely incurable genre," he wrote in a letter of 1855. After Baudelaire's death in 1867, his old mentor, Théophile Gautier, wrote an introduction to the first volume of Baudelaire's collected works, in which he observed: "All sensation becomes for him the motif of an analysis. Involuntarily, he doubles himself and, lacking any other subject, becomes the spy of himself."[21] This doubling, this split within the self, this taste for inner struggle Baudelaire alternately viewed as a boon and as a damnation for the artist. "The poet enjoys the incomparable privilege of being able to be at once himself and someone else," he says in "Les foules" (Le Spleen *de Paris).* And in his earliest serious consideration of Delacroix in the "Salon de 1846," he wrote: "For a man like this, endowed with such courage and passion, the most interesting struggles are those which he has to maintain against himself."[22] In his poems, on the other hand, the word "irony" stands in high relief, intimating the foreordained defeat of the artist — the *modern* artist — in his search for universal harmony. Since Baudelaire was well educated in the classics and a great frequenter of dictionaries where etymological roots were given, his use of the word "irony" naturally carried within it the original meaning of the Greek *eiron:* the dissembler of speech, the character in the Greek drama who knew, but pretended he knew not; he who, like Socrates, simulated ignorance for the purpose of revealing a truth. However the word is used by Baudelaire, it is always a signal of his keenest feelings of wrenching duality and malaise. "Ne suis-je pas un faux accord / Dans la divine symphonie, / Grâce à la vorace Ironie / Qui me secoue et qui me mord?" ("Am I not a false accord in the divine symphony, thanks to voracious Irony that jolts and consumes me?") he asks in "Héautontimorouménos" ("Self-Tormenter"). In "L'Irrémédiable" he defines the terrible state of the poet who experienced the dark tête-à-tête "Qu'un cœur devenu son miroir" ("of a heart that has become its own mirror"). In this poem, an infernal, ironic beacon is seen like a pale star, evoking one side of the poet's secret life — his *consciousness* of evil.

"Consciousness," that most modern of words, became ubiquitous in Baudelaire's century, when psychology was already wearing away classic categories and when the "I" and "non-I" were already interiorized: consciousness rose to stand self-consciously at the beginning of modernism. Baudelaire's preoccupation with consciousness was accompanied by two other heightened experiences: the sense of otherness and the sense of unremitting doubt. Baudelaire presented otherness both in its psychological guise, later codified by Freud (the alter ego), and in its purest literary form, as allegory. He very specifically restored allegory, which had lost its ground with moderns of his period, bearing in mind its root in the Greek *allos,* other, as a legitimate poetic mode, turning it in the direction that could easily be adapted by the later Symbolists, with their notion of prolonged, hidden metaphor, and by twentieth-century moderns who, like Joyce, would tell of a self, of many selfs, in extended allegory. Baudelaire's own stories, such as "La Chambre double" ("The Double Chamber") in *Le Spleen de Paris,* are often allegories of his condition as artist.

Doubt slips easily into this atmosphere of dreadful tensions and dualities. In his 1846 "Salon," Baudelaire had belabored painters without commitments, who were eclectics because they were doubters and therefore begged the aid of all the other arts. "Experiment with the contradictory means, the encroachment of one art upon another, the importation of poetry, wit, and sentiment into painting — all these modern miseries are vices peculiar to the eclectics."[23] Decades later, Nietzsche would echo him. Doubt and skepticism as characteristic of the modern grew in Baudelaire's œuvre as he himself became more and more prey to them. After he had wholeheartedly thrown himself into the commitments of a political idealist, for instance, at the time of the revolution of 1848, he experienced the bitter aftermath and turned away from all Utopian blueprints. He was better able to understand Delacroix in his last essay after these experiences; Delacroix, who believed that nothing changed in politics, was sarcastic about "childish Utopian enthusiasms" and had the "zest of incredulity."[24]

When Christopher Isherwood wrote an introduction to the republication, in 1947, of his translation of *Journaux intimes,* he ruefully commented, "After two world wars and the atomic bomb, we of today should understand him better than his contemporaries." Although Baudelaire despised in himself his incurable, mordant irony and even satirized himself as Hamlet, "cet histrion en vacances" ("this actor on vacation"), a ridiculously doubt-ridden figure, in "La Béatrice," he nonetheless regarded doubt as the natural concomitant of the "more abstract" character of modern urban life. Even what he called "the heroism of modern life" unfolded under its aegis. Finally, all this doubt and irony arrive at what Octavio Paz has again and again located as the modern aesthetic hallmark: critical consciousness. Despite his own reservation about certain of Baudelaire's poems that, he says, reflect "the bad taste of the times," Paz has rendered homage to Baudelaire's critical insights and reflects them in his own critical writing:

> Modernity represents the rule of criticism: not a system, but the negation and confrontation of all systems. Criticism has been the staple nourishment of all modern artists.[25]

And even those modern writers who, like Albert Camus, wistfully transformed some of Baudelaire's thoughts — for instance, when he re-forms Baudelaire's famous lines about the equivalence multitude-solitude into solitude-solidarity — knew, best of all, the Baudelairean power of negation.

Our notion of the avant-garde is rooted in Baudelaire, although he himself sarcastically remarked the propensity for military metaphors in France, where "every metaphor wears mustaches" (1:690). The spirit of revolt, defiance, and separation has informed art from Baudelaire's day — Courbet to Manet — to our own. Artists have been inspired by Baudelaire's often enigmatic statements, by his philosophic musings (Gauguin), by his unflinching realism (Rodin and Cézanne), by his phantasmagoric visions (Redon), by his authentic religiosity (Rouault), by his incomparable descriptions of the real transformed into the strange (Magritte). Critics have been fueled by his critical principles — his unwillingness to be trapped in a system — by his insistence on passion and partiality, by his conversational tone, and, above all, by his cosmopolitanism. They have learned to understand that faced with new experiences, or the experiences of art from other cultures, "the critic, the spectator," must "work a transformation in himself."[26] In the twentieth century critics have had repeated recourse to Baudelaire's thoughts, often in spite of themselves, under protest, and in an avant-garde spirit of defiance. Check the index of any considerable body of work by an established art critic in our century, and Baudelaire invariably appears, often rather often. He was himself a "beacon," whose lamp has not dimmed (although it has sometimes been obscured, as both lamp and voyagers turn in the twentieth century's night).

After the first generation of twentieth-century modern artists, there was a lull in response to Baudelaire's prompting; but a new generation appeared in whom Baudelaire flowered yet again, under the energetic leadership of poet-critics, first among them André Breton. Like Picasso, he recognized Baudelaire's paternity, not only of his most cherished forebears, Arthur Rimbaud and the Comte de Lautréamont, but also of the visual artists of his time. The important words at the end of the synoptic poem "Le Voyage" — so important they threaten to become unexamined modern clichés — operated strongly on the Surrealists: "Plonger au fond du gouffre, Enfer ou Ciel, qu'importe? / Au fond de l'Inconnu pour trouver du *nouveau!* ("To plunge into the depths of the abyss, Hell or Heaven, what does it matter? To the depths of the Unknown in order to find something *new!*") When Breton first wrote about Max Ernst, for instance, he said Ernst had "plunged into the unknown'' and had later obeyed Baudelaire's injunction to ''search for the new.'' When he wrote shortly after about Giorgio de Chirico, he said that it was in Chirico's square, ''where everything seems so close to existence and yet bears so little resemblance to what really exists,'' that he and his generation held their ''invisible meetings.'' He spoke of Chirico's city — as self-contained as a rampart and lit from within itself — in which he tried to get his bearings and to work out ''the far from alternating rising and setting of the suns of the mind.''[27] Baudelaire's thrumming rhythms saturate Breton's prose and sometimes his poetry. But so do the images, or, rather, the leitmotifs, for among Breton's most compelling themes linger Baudelaire's signposts pointing to the unknown.

Breton, Louis Aragon, Paul Eluard, and Benjamin Péret — poets who doubled as art critics — were all extravagantly enchanted by Baudelaire's enchanted mirror and his ''anguish of curiosity'' (''L'Invitation au voyage''). Above all, they courted the experience of the marvelous, its shocking surprise, so often evoked by Baudelaire and likened to the dream. When Baudelaire struggled to describe Delacroix's specialty, he asked: How is it he produces a sensation of novelty? His answer:

> He expresses above all the innermost atmosphere of the brain, the astonishing aspect of things. . . . It is the infinite in the finite. It is a dream! And I don't mean by that word the jumbled places of the night, but the vision produced by intense meditation. [2:636–637]

The dream, as every Surrealist knew, was the natural habitat of the marvelous and also, as Baudelaire said, the burden of the traveler to the unknown, whose ''singular fortune'' was to find his goal always receding and, ''being nowhere, can be anywhere'' (''Le Voyage''). The Surrealists found themselves, and the works of their most admired visual artists, in that no place, suspended between dream and reality, that they insisted they would bring to the same place, onto the same plane. They were like ''Ceux-là dont les désirs ont la forme des nues, / Et qui rêvent, ainsi qu'un conscrit le canon, / De vastes voluptés, changeantes, inconnues, / Et dont l'esprit humain n'a jamais su le nom!'' (''Those whose desires have the form of clouds, and who dream, as the conscript dreams of the cannon, of vast, changing, unknown raptures whose name the human spirit has never known!''; ''Le Voyage''). Sleep is full of miracles, as Baudelaire said in ''Rêve parisien'' (''Parisian Dream'').

The elements of shock and surprise were closely identified with chance in the Surrealist mind. The marvelous would never show itself to the pedant nor to those whose recourse to reason was unreasonable — all those professors whom Baudelaire despised (2:657; ''Erudition serves to disguise the absence of imagination''; ''Salon de 1859''). Baudelaire, and his sons among the Surrealists, believed fervently in giving his soul — all its poetry — ''à l'inconnu qui passe'' (''to the unexpected as it comes along''; ''Les foules,'' Le Spleen de Paris). He named the immensity of the sky and sea, solitude, silence, and the incomparable chastity of the blue as ''choses pensent par moi, ou je pense par elles (car dans la grandeur de la rêverie, le moi se perd vite!)'' (''things that think through me or I through them [since in the grandeur of reverie the I is quickly lost!]'') and hastened to add: ''elles pensent, dis-je, mais musicalement et pittoresquement, sans arguties, sans syllogismes, sans déductions'' (''they think, I say, but musically, and picturesquely, without cavils, without syllogisms, without deductions''; ''Le Confiteor de l'artiste'').

Baudelaire was the direct source of the Surrealists' obsession with the city. They were all flaneurs. Both Louis Aragon in his novel The Peasant of Paris and Breton in his novel Nadja moved through Paris exactly as Baudelaire directed, seeing strangeness in everyday objects; violence in urban change (alas, said Baudelaire, the city changes more quickly than the human heart); the tragic and sometimes the bizarre in the lives of its denizens; lights in midnight chambers inspiring magical conjectures; the sinister and beautiful in its dusks and dawns. Like Baudelaire they had their doubts about progress, which he said was like the scorpion that sticks itself with its own tail, and they turned back, far back, to primitive cultures, seeking the truths that modern technology had papered over. All the same, the city, that prodigy reflecting the modern drive, was their pasture, the source of their inspired moments, as well as their nemesis. Just as Baudelaire drew upon the *faits divers* of Parisian life in his prose poems, so the Surrealists incorporated lurid squibs from daily newspapers, giving them a dimension Baudelaire would have recognized — a dimension born of irony.

In 1944 Breton identified a brewing quarrel between those artists who were determined to retain direct contact with the outer world, although radically modifying it, and those who demanded independence from the restrictions of conventional space and thought that the picture should draw its objective value from itself alone. He called them two reefs and recommended that agreement be reached on the basis of Baudelaire's proposals, which he quoted:

> All the faculties of the human soul must be subordinated to the imagination, which requisitions them simultaneously. . . . Both line and color inspire thoughts and dreams; the pleasures derived from them are each of a different nature, yet perfectly equal and absolutely independent of the subject of the picture.[28]

Perhaps, as he praised Kandinsky, Breton, who knew his Baudelaire by heart, remembered Baudelaire's passage in "Fusées":

> I believe that the infinite and mysterious charm that lies in the contemplation of a ship, above all a ship in motion, depends first upon its order and symmetry, which are primordial needs of the human spirit as great as those of intricacy and harmony — and, second, upon the successive multiplication and generation of all the curves and imaginary figures described in space by the real elements of the object.
>
> The poetic idea that emerges from this operation of line in motion is a hypothesis of an immeasurably vast, complex, yet perfectly harmonized entity, of an animal full of genius, suffering and sighing all the ambitions of men. [1:663–664]

But harmony, the ideal, was only one side of the story. The Surrealist conception of beauty was as violent, as fraught with shocking imagery, as Baudelaire's own — a thrust of the dagger against the hypocrite reader and viewer. Beauty, Breton blared, would be convulsive, or it would not be. His colleague Paul Eluard, in the first number of *Minotaure* in 1933, writing on Matisse's portrait of Baudelaire, called his essay "The Mirror of Baudelaire," remembering Baudelaire's many allusions to his own dark, often tarnished mirror. "All the powers of unhappiness are lined up in his corner," Eluard wrote, and said that it was the taste for unhappiness that made him eminently modern. Writing at a moment of profound crisis in France, Eluard saw in Baudelaire's "untarnished" mirror his own epoch: "In an epoch in which the sense of the word happiness is degraded day by day to the point of becoming synonymous with unconsciousness, this fatal taste [for unhappiness] is the surpassing virtue of Baudelaire." Still, he singled out Baudelaire's pride as his enduring characteristic and admired his definition of the dandy as the defender of opposition and revolt, of "all that is best in human pride."

The "fatal taste" made its presence felt in the Western Hemisphere as well. If Baudelaire was companionable for circumstantial reasons during the troubled 1930s in Paris, he was being rediscovered at the same time by countless artists and writers equally uneasy in the Americas, particularly in the United States. During the Depression years a small but distinctive group of visual artists fiercely resisted the social demands of the period. Aspiring to cosmopolitanism, they found their way to Baudelaire. An edition of his poetry and prose, published in 1919, was kept in print, and many painters had it in their studios. Wary of provincialism, they foraged among those journals that honored internationalism, where they found articles about, and new translations of, Baudelaire. Christopher Isherwood's translation of *Journaux intimes* of 1930 carried T. S. Eliot's introduction. Americans with vanguard ambitions were very well aware of Eliot's importance to their position. A surprising number of painters were more than casually acquainted with his work. Despite Eliot's reservations about Baudelaire's poetry, he, too, was in thrall to the rhythms, intonations — the breath — and above all, his irony, which infiltrates Eliot's own work even in the later poems of the *Four Quartets*. How much they sound the rhythms and spirit of Baudelaire's "L'Héautontimorouménos":

> Je suis la plaie et le couteau!
> Je suis le soufflet et la joue!
> Je suis les membres et la roue,
> Et la victime et le bourreau!
>
> I am the wound and the knife!
> I am the slap and the cheek!
> I am the dismembered limbs and the wheel,
> And the victim and the executioner!

As the 1930s shaded into the 1940s, a feeling of impasse, of aesthetic despair, overtook American painters who had experienced so many ethical, political, and aesthetic conflicts. Arshile Gorky, a leader in the avant-garde, gloomily told his confreres, "Let's face it, we're bankrupt."[29] Others described in published statements a pro-

found sense of disarray. With fair frequency during the 1940s these painters expressed in their works and words a desire to flee anywhere out of this world. The image of flight, seen as spiritual voyage, held great allure for them. In their disaffection from American materialism, and their view of technological progress as responsible for the hideous machinery of the Second World War, they, like Baudelaire, moved far away from the quotidian, often to the distant horizons of ancient myths.

One of the younger animators of the American avant-garde of the period, Robert Motherwell, had familiarized himself with Baudelaire in 1937, when, at the age of twenty-two, he was writing his thesis on Delacroix. Echoes of Baudelaire occurred persistently in his subsequent writings. In the Winter 1944 issue of *Partisan Review,* for instance, he chose a telling epigraph from Baudelaire's "Le *Confiteor* de l'artiste": "L'étude du beau est un duel où l'artiste crie de frayeur avant d'être vaincu" ("The study of the beautiful is a duel in which the artist cries out in terror before he is vanquished"). Two years later, writing in *Design* in April, he titles his essay "Beyond the Aesthetic" and opens with: "For the goal which lies beyond the strictly aesthetic the French artists say the 'unknown' or the 'new' after Baudelaire and Rimbaud." With the clear memory of Baudelaire in mind, Motherwell writes that the function of the aesthetic "becomes that of a medium, a means for getting at the infinite background of feeling in order to condense it into an object of perception." In 1949, writing an introduction to Marcel Raymond's *From Baudelaire to Surrealism,* which, as director of Documents of Modern Art, a series of essential books on modernism, he had arranged to have published, he again opens with an epigraph from Baudelaire: "The arts aspire, if not to complement one another, at least to lend one another new energies." Motherwell's abiding

4 Robert Motherwell
The Voyage, 1949

interest in Baudelaire was stimulated by his concourse with the Surrealists, many of whom found refuge in New York during the Second World War, as well as by his working relationship with the critic Harold Rosenberg, who, like Motherwell, carried his deep impressions of Baudelaire's poetry and, above all, his art criticism, into his entire œuvre. Even his first important art critical book in 1959 was explicitly titled *The Tradition of the New.*

Motherwell's sustained attention to Baudelaire led him to paint a key work in 1949 titled *The Voyage,* directly inspired by Baudelaire's poem. He recapitulated the theme some years later in *The Voyage Ten Years After.* The earlier version assembled emphatic, flat signs, in measured movement and horizontal progression, in a clear light, suggesting endless displacement. Motherwell reflects the youngish protagonist in Baudelaire's early stanzas, who leaves simply in order to leave and is still in love with maps and prints. In the second version the voice is more ambiguous. The pale light Motherwell establishes as the dominant tone suggests Baudelaire's sad reference in later stanzas to the Eldorados the Imagination calls up, only to find "un récif aux clartés du matin" ("a mere sandbar in the morning light"). The forms in Motherwell's later *Voyage* are equivocal, both

menacing and soft, as are Baudelaire's images of clouds, reflecting "l'attrait mystérieux / De ceux que le hasard fait avec les nuages" ("the mysterious attraction chance creates with clouds"). A sensed irony tinges the whole painting, as though Motherwell had grown to agree with the poet and see himself as the brother Baudelaire addresses, who finds the beautiful in everything that comes from far off. The spumy texture of the main figure bespeaks an artist who had learned the extreme nuances of form, and, as Baudelaire said in *Journaux intimes,* had understood that "form is independent of matter: molecules do not constitute form" (1:705).

Motherwell was not the only painter of his generation to be directly inspired by Baudelaire. His friend William Baziotes had discovered the poet before he was twenty and would never forsake the atmosphere, the "livery," of the ensemble of Baudelaire's poetry. To Baziotes, Baudelaire's voice spoke in a timbre known to him, whose own surprisingly romantic temperament unashamedly followed its own star, as Baziotes said each artist must do. Baziotes often drew directly upon specific poems in *Les Fleurs du mal,* such as "Le Balcon" ("The Balcony") and "Correspondances," but he also fused images dispersed throughout Baudelaire's poems, such as those of the sea and moon — the sea above all. An aquatic atmosphere, with all its wavering light and mottled depths, suffuses his entire œuvre, responding to so many of Baudelaire's poems but perhaps most of all to the prose poem "Les Bienfaits de la lune" ("Favors of the Moon") in *Le Spleen de Paris,* which Baziotes's widow reported was his favorite. Baudelaire says the moon fills the room with an "atmosphère phosphorique" ("phosphorescent light") that speaks of water, clouds, silence, and the night, and, above all, of the immense green sea with "l'eau informe et multiforme" ("water without form and multiform"). The very feel of the things Baudelaire names is the subject of Baziotes's œuvre.

Baziotes and Motherwell alluded directly to Baudelaire, but others of their friends in the Abstract Expressionist group were less specific. Still, the tremors of the poet and critic touched them all. One of their most firmly stated beliefs had been deposited by Baudelaire in the lore of modern painting: the importance of the subject. While the poet was aware of the artist's necessity to abstract form from subject matter, he also paradoxically defined the artist's right and duty to have a subject — a subtle distinction:

> I can never consider the choice of subject as a matter of indifference, and that in spite of the necessary love that must enrich the most humble fragment, I believe the subject works for the artist as part of his genius, and for me — a barbarian after all — as part of my pleasure. [2:668, "Salon de 1859"]

The Abstract Expressionists could not have agreed more fervently. In their famous letter to the *New York Times* published on June 13, 1943, Adolph Gottlieb and Mark Rothko commenced with a Baudelairean definition of art as "an adventure into an unknown world." They then stated:

It is a widely accepted notion among painters that it does not matter what one paints as long as it is well painted. This is the essence of academicism. There is no such thing as good painting about nothing. We assert that the subject is crucial and only that subject-matter is valid which is tragic and timeless.

Rothko, who often felt himself to be "within two steps of the abyss," as Baudelaire said every mystic is, later painted subjects as abstract, as evanescent, as Baudelaire's skies, seas, dawns, and dusks — allegories. Of all the painters of his generation, he was, by temperament, most available to Baudelaire's central notion of correspondence and, above all, to the power of music to inform his painting. The spaces Baudelaire evinced in his discussion of music in the essays on Wagner — he said he felt himself "released from the bonds of gravity" and felt "space reaching to the fullest conceivable limits" — were familiar to Rothko and others of his generation, as was Wagner's idea, quoted by Baudelaire, of a "new concatenation of the phenomena of the world which the eyes could not perceive in the ordinary state of waking."[30]

5 Robert Motherwell
The Voyage Ten Years After,
1961

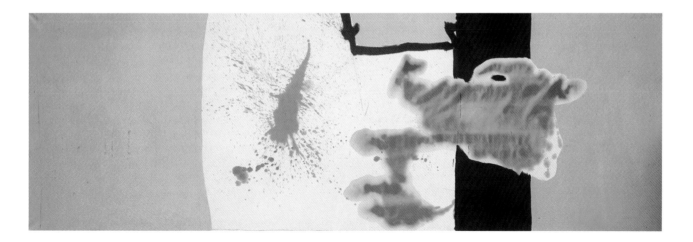

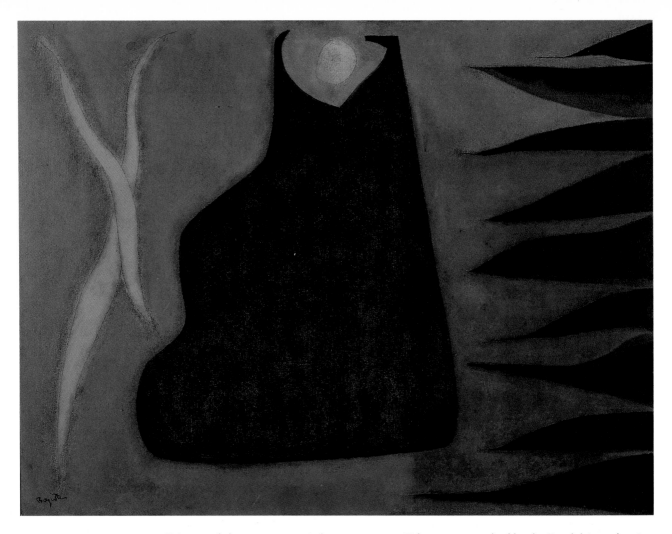

6 William Baziotes
Trance, 1953

Painters of the postwar period were peculiarly susceptible to Baudelaire's idea of "the concordant parts of all the arts and the similarities in their methods," an idea that appeared both in his essay "L'Œuvre et la vie d'Eugène Delacroix" and in the discussion of Wagner's "coincidence of several arts." In subsequent generations these ideas would be translated into happenings, installation art, and performance art. Some artists of Rothko's generation, such as Arshile Gorky and Mark Tobey, were touched by the Baudelairean longing to merge with the universe; by "nature," which they saw as speaking to and through them in confused symbols (correspondences). These murmurings were interpreted in abstractions. Other artists, such as Willem de Kooning, were more available to the mysterious charms of urban clutter, first introduced by Baudelaire as suitable subject matter for the modern poet and painter. Still others carried through Baudelaire's demands for drama in landscape painting, moving away, as did Clyfford Still, from representation. "Most of our landscape painters are liars," Baudelaire said in his "Salon de 1859," initiating a paradox still active in aesthetic theory by adding that they were liars "precisely because they neglected to lie" (2:668). Picasso would reiterate the message when he said that art is a lie that reveals the truth.

Wherever we look in that audacious postwar generation, we find reverberations of Baudelaire's modernism, even if sometimes the artists themselves were unaware of the origins of their musings. Baudelaire's shade often hovers behind the unsuspecting artist. The marked preoccupation with the void, the abyss, nothingness that reappears throughout the Western world after the Second World War owes its embodiment to Baudelaire. Did Sartre, who so much influenced painters and sculptors after the war, realize he had been living through Baudelaire, who had early been embossed on his spirit, when he wrote that for months he came and went with the abyss (le gouffre) at his side? This paraphrase of one of Baudelaire's most arresting opening lines — "Pascal avait son gouffre, avec lui se mouvant" ("Pascal had his abyss, moving with him") — moved with Sartre as he turned to art criticism; when, for instance, he defined Giacometti through the ineluctable presence of the void in his work. Even in places such as Eastern Europe, isolated after the Second World War, Baudelaire was retrieved and found new expression through works such as the hybrids of the Czech artist Jiři Kolář. Not only was Kolář inspired by specific poems, but his whole way of thinking was tempered by his knowledge of Baudelaire, whose psychological climate is reflected in Kolář's statement:

> Art has nothing whatever to do with what is private or public, political or poetic, beautiful or ugly, everyday or absurd, nude or symbolic, but with a domain in which the private and public, the polit-

ical and poetic, the beautiful and ugly, the everyday and absurd, the nude and the symbolic, are indissociable — of a domain in which beauty and death, history and nature, fantasy and reality, dream and memory are inseparable.[31]

Today, perhaps, no one is content to be irremediably modern. A certain dissociation has muffled Baudelaire's voice among intellectuals, but the spirit of revolt is certainly still with us, and the abyss, undeniably, still moves with us.

7 Mark Rothko
No. 117, 1961

8 Georges Rouault
Portrait of Charles Baude-laire, c. 1924–1927

Beacons

A story, perhaps apocryphal, is told of Michelangelo. The painter cherished his copy of Dante's *Divine Comedy* more than any other earthly possession. While reading it he made sketches inspired by Dante's poetry in the margins. When Pope Julius II summoned the painter to Rome to begin work on the ceiling of the Sistine Chapel, Michelangelo packed his treasure in a trunk that was to be shipped by sea while he traveled to Rome by land. The ship went down in a storm and with it the illustrated *Divine Comedy*. Feeling the loss most keenly, the artist decided to elaborate on the drawings — on the ceiling of the Sistine Chapel. Thus the greatest frescoes ever painted were inspired by one of the greatest poems ever written.

The question of how one art form inspires or influences another has prompted considerable debate through the ages. Much of the discussion focuses on poetry and painting, which in the eighteenth century were often called "the sister arts." As far back as the fifth century B.C. Simonides of Ceos said, "painting is mute poetry and poetry a speaking picture." The Roman poet Horace declared "ut pictura poesis" ("as a painting, so also a poem"), and although he probably meant only that both poems and paintings deserve respect and close study, his phrase has become a point of departure for those who claim that a special relationship exists between these two art forms.

The poetry of Charles Baudelaire provides a unique window into the realm where the spectacle of one art form inspiring another unfolds. Not only is Baudelaire regarded by many as the greatest poet of nineteenth-century France, he is acknowledged as its greatest art critic as well. His deep involvement in visual art, his variegated artistic temperament, and his appearance at a crucial time make his responses to art and the response of artists to his poetry a seedbed for cross-fertilization of art forms. Baudelaire, who was born in 1821, developed his appreciation for the arts at a time when Romanticism had moved out of the avant-garde into the mainstream of art and literature, and his own work could be termed a summation of it. He was, however, not without his classical tendencies, especially in his craft as a poet; and he is often viewed as the precursor of Symbolism and indeed of modernism itself. Thus, like Manet, he was a bridge between periods. Generation after generation of modern artists has been moved enough by his art criticism and his poetry to consider him its forerunner.

The voyages in the title of this book are metaphorical journeys of exploration. In his poems Baudelaire, who rarely ventured beyond Paris, travels "sans vapeur et sans voile" (1:131; "without steam and without sail") into human consciousness. To make this poetic exploration, he repeatedly employed the motif of the voyage. Among his most celebrated poems are "L'Invitation au voyage" ("Invitation to the Voyage"), "Moesta et errabunda" ("Sad and Wandering"), "Bohémiens en voyage" ("Gypsies Traveling"), and "Le Voyage," his longest poem, the reprise for his only volume of verse poetry, *Les Fleurs du mal* (*The Flowers of Evil*).

Baudelaire's life was an aggregation of contradictions, all of which informed the paradoxical complexity of his poetry. His personae included the top-hatted dandy and the tormented soul, the voluptuary and the obsessive perfectionist, the petulant child and the worshiper of childlike naïveté, the flaneur and the serious intellectual, the effete poet and the advocate of hard work and discipline, the man with an abiding passion for those who suffer in the confined streets of the city and the dreamer who pursued boundlessly the pathways of his imagination.

In his voyages in poetry as well as in life, Baudelaire often descended into the darkness of his soul, where he almost always discovered the devil encouraging his own natural depravity, a condition he considered universal. He believed in the notion of original sin with an insistent certainty, contrary to the ideas of his century with its romantic notions about the basic goodness of man and its increasing faith in the power of science to produce progress. For Baudelaire, progress could not come through the invention of the balloon or the bicycle, gas lights or steam turbines, but only through a lessening of original sin. And for most of his life he did not believe even that was possible. He saw the human condition as irreparable. When Gustave Flaubert complained to him that "you have (and repeatedly) insisted too much (?) on the 'spirit of evil,'"[1] Baudelaire replied, "I was struck by your observation and, having very sincerely descended into the memory of my reveries, I realized that I've always been obsessed by the impossibility of understanding certain of man's sudden thoughts or deeds, unless we accept the hypothesis that an evil force, external to man, has intervened. Now that's a great admission that the whole of the nineteenth century couldn't conspire to make me blush at."[2] From the beginning of Les Fleurs du mal in the poem "Au Lecteur" ("To the Reader") to the poem he designated for its conclusion, "Le Voyage," Baudelaire makes frequent journeys into a heart of darkness where evil, whether innate or exterior, is the force that controls the destiny of human beings.

Baudelaire's favorite real journey was the one that took him out of his hotel room or garret — he was peripatetic, moving from one very humble abode to another, often to avoid creditors — into the streets of Paris, where he observed the beau monde on the boulevards and in the parks, the artists and writers in their cafés, and the poor and suffering in the narrow and twisting streets. In many of his city poems there is a tension between his concrete observations of the city, even his celebration of it, and his abiding belief in the depravity of the soul. The contrast between his fascination with the constantly unfolding newness of modern life manifested in the city and the constancy of the depraved human condition parading there is what makes his poetry play such a significant role in the development of the modern sensibility. In his poetic lament for the old city of Paris that was disappearing before his eyes, he writes, ". . . La forme d'une ville / Change plus vite, hélas! que le cœur d'un mortel" (1:85; ". . . The form of a city changes faster, alas! than the heart of a mortal").

His "voyages into the city" produce some of the most vivid and telling images in his poetry. These urban word pictures are particularly prominent in the chapter entitled "Tableaux parisiens" ("Paris Pictures") added to the second edition of Les Fleurs du mal in 1861 and in his volume of prose poems sometimes called Le Spleen de Paris (Paris Spleen),[3] which was not published as a book until after his death. In the preface to that volume he described his poems as coming "above all from frequenting enormous cities, from the crossroads of their innumerable interrelations" (1:276).

At those moments when journeys into the city, into an exterior world of disorder, seemed unsatisfying or even unbearable, Baudelaire retreated to the solitude of his attic room, to an enclosed interior. A voice would call to him, "'Viens! oh! viens voyager dans les rêves, / Au-delà du possible, au-delà du connu!'" (1:170; "'Come! oh! come voyage in dreams, beyond the possible, beyond the known!'"), and he would embark upon a third voyage, the "voyage into the dream." The word rêve (dream), or some form of it, appears repeatedly in his poetry, and some of his most beautiful and startling poems evoke or seek a dream state. Sometimes these dreams were induced by hashish or opium. He was addicted to the latter in the form of laudanum, which he took to escape the ravages of both syphilis and life. His poetry, however, was not a form of escape. There he created dreams of ecstasy but never denied life's nightmares. In his art, he faced life squarely.

Sometimes the dreams focused on worldly paradises: sumptuous boudoirs where the terrors of the world fade in a haze of eroticism and sensuality; tropical paradises replete with images from his only genuine voyage — an aborted journey to India when he was twenty that terminated on the island of Mauritius; oriental paradises emerging from his reading and from his collection of Japanese prints; a northern European paradise, based on his love for the intriguing combination of the exotic and the orderly in the seventeenth-century Dutch paintings he so favored in his trips to the Louvre and other galleries in Paris. At other times the world, even as it appeared in his dreams, seemed to hold no promise at all. In one of his prose poems he acknowledges the paradox of wanting to be anywhere but where he is. His soul tells him to go "'N'importe où! n'importe où! pourvu que ce soit hors de ce monde!'" (1:357; "'anywhere, anywhere, provided it is outside of this world!'") Sometimes his dreams led only into the abyss and became another voyage into the depths. Sometimes they ventured back into the chaotic nightmare of the swarming city, and sometimes they recreated the city as a realm of perfection. Sometimes these dreams were a trip into the horrors of his life and sometimes a means of escape from them. In a sense all of his poetry is the product of his experience reshaped by his imagination and his dreams. As critic Martin Turnell commented, "With Baudelaire every poem

is a voyage — an interior voyage — of discovery and he does not know where he is going until the end of the journey."[4] Baudelaire himself wrote, "Poetry is what is more than real; it is what is only completely true in *another world*"(2:59).

That other world is the world of artistic creation, the world where "toutes ces choses pensent

9 Emile Deroy
Portrait of Charles Baudelaire, 1844

10 Henri Fantin-Latour
Hommage à Delacroix,
1864

Among those paying
homage to Delacroix are
James McNeill Whistler
(standing to the left of the
portrait), Edouard Manet
(standing to the right of
the portrait), Henri Fantin-
Latour (seated, coatless),
and Baudelaire (seated,
far right).

par moi, ou je pense par elles (car dans la grandeur de la rêverie, le *moi* se perd vite!); elles pensent, dis-je, mais musicalement et pittoresquement, sans arguties, sans syllogismes, sans déductions'' (1:278; ''all these things thinking through me or I through them (since in the grandeur of reverie, the *I* is quickly lost!); they think, as I say, but in music and in the picturesque, without arguments, without syllogisms, without deductions.'' And it is this other world, the world where ''le *moi*'' is lost and replaced by art, that is the province of another of Baudelaire's voyages, the ''voyage into the new.'' Baudelaire wrote that imagination, for him ''the queen of the faculties,'' the sine qua non of all great art, ''decomposes all creation, and with the raw materials accumulated and disposed in accordance with rules whose origins one cannot find save in the furthest depths of the soul, it creates a new world, it produces the sensation of newness.''[5] All of Baudelaire's poetry then

becomes a voyage ''Au fond de l'Inconnu pour trouver *du nouveau!*'' (1:134; ''On to the depths of the Unknown to find something *new!*''). The only means of combating the human condition is to create a separate world of art that simultaneously contains the original world *and* is something new as well. This art both recognizes and flies in the face of irreparable depravity by reshaping it in a poem. For Baudelaire poetry is not a superficial escape but a form of alchemy, a way, as he put it, of ''transforming mud into gold'' (1:188). From poetry came ''l'esprit de l'ordre qui crée la liberté'' (''the spirit of order that creates liberty'').[6] This liberty becomes a springboard from which other poets and painters can leap into the new. Nothing could reveal more about Baudelaire's extraordinary place in the creation of modernism than this imperative for newness that emerges from his poetry — paradoxically coupled with his constant attempts to recapture the past.

Like poetry, painting also had for Baudelaire the power to control reality, to shape it, and to give it form. As "a section of the sky seen through a ventilator or between two chimneys, two rocks, or through an arcade, etc., gives a more profound idea of the infinite than a great panorama seen from a mountain top,"[7] so a painting could contain "l'infini dans le fini" (2:636; "the infinite within the finite") and could within its boundaries exercise control over the otherwise uncontrollable variables in life at the same time it reflected them with penetrating clarity. Like poetry, painting was a means of expressing in an exterior form what occurred during the interior journey. What he called "my great, my unique, my primitive passion" (1:701) for pictures began when he was quite young. "Even in my extreme youth my eyes had never been able to drink their fill of painted or sculpted images," he wrote in the "Salon de 1859."[8] After a school trip to Versailles when he was seventeen, he emphasized only two things in a letter to his stepfather, meeting the king and giving his opinion about the pictures he saw in the galleries. He didn't like many of them and had little trouble knowing why: "All the paintings made during the Empire which are supposed to be very beautiful often seem so regular, so cold. The people in them are frequently arranged like trees, or minor characters in an opera. It's probably very silly of me to talk in this way of paintings that have been so highly praised; perhaps I'm speaking nonsense, but I'm only giving my own impressions."[9] The advocate of the painting of modern life was already in evidence long before he launched his career as an art critic in 1845.

By the time he was nineteen and living on his own in the Latin Quarter, he spent a substantial amount of his allowance buying prints and paintings, a habit that started him down the road of indebtedness on which he stayed for the rest of his life. In the early 1840s he lived in the Hôtel Pimodan on the Ile Saint-Louis, a mansion turned apartment house that was famous for its history as well as for its resident bohemians and dandies. On the walls of his room Baudelaire hung an impressive number of pictures. Most prominent was a portrait of himself by his friend Emile Deroy (FIG. 9), which is the only picture of Baudelaire from this time of his life — and perhaps the only portrait of him in which contentment is the dominant trait. Many of the other pictures were copies of works by artists such as Tintoretto, Correggio, Nicolas Poussin, and Diego Velázquez.[10] The work of a contemporary, however, dominated his quarters as well as his taste. From the moment he saw The Justice of Trajan at the Louvre in 1840, Eugène Delacroix (1798–1863) became his hero. For Baudelaire, Delacroix was "one of the rare elect" among artists, the equivalent in his own age of the Renaissance masters and "the model of the painter-poet."[11] A print of The Women of Algiers, an oil painting entitled Sorrow, and the entire set of lithographs illustrating Hamlet were early purchases of the poet.

It was not long before Baudelaire's devotion to poetry and painting led to an image from a visual work of art finding its way into one of his poems. In 1843 his jealousy was aroused by an unpleasant episode with Jeanne Duval, the woman with whom he would have a tortured but devoted relationship throughout most of his adult life (FIG. 27). The result was the poem "La Béatrice," which contains an interesting correspondence to one or more of the lithographs from the Delacroix Hamlet series. In the poem, a pack of imaginary fiends are taunting the jilted poet. They say, "— 'Contemplons à loisir cette caricature / Et cette ombre d'Hamlet imitant sa posture, / Le regard indécis et les cheveux au vent'" ("— 'Let us consider at our leisure this caricature, this shadow of a Hamlet, imitating his posture, his indecisive gaze, his hair in the wind'"). The lithograph depicting Hamlet following his father's ghost (FIG. 11) was probably hanging not far from Baudelaire's writing table while he was composing the poem.[12]

There can be no doubt how much these *Hamlet* lithographs affected the poet. In a later critical essay he wrote, "They are so deeply moving and attractive that once it has bathed in their little worlds of melancholy, the eye can no longer escape them, and the mind is forever in their thrall. 'And once left, the picture torments and follows us.'"[13] He was pursued by the image of

LA BÉATRICE

Dans des terrains cendreux, calcinés, sans verdure,
Comme je me plaignais un jour à la nature,
Et que de ma pensée, en vaguant au hasard,
J'aiguisais lentement sur mon cœur le poignard,
Je vis en plein midi descendre sur ma tête
Un nuage funèbre et gros d'une tempête,
Qui portait un troupeau de démons vicieux,
Semblables à des nains cruels et curieux.
A me considérer froidement ils se mirent,
Et, comme des passants sur un fou qu'ils admirent,
Je les entendis rire et chuchoter entre eux,
En échangeant maint signe et maint clignement
            d'yeux:

— "Contemplons à loisir cette caricature
Et cette ombre d'Hamlet imitant sa posture,
Le regard indécis et les cheveux au vent.
N'est-ce pas grand'pitié de voir ce bon vivant,
Ce gueux, cet histrion en vacances, ce drôle,
Parce qu'il sait jouer artistement son rôle,
Vouloir intéresser au chant de ses douleurs
Les aigles, les grillons, les ruisseaux et les fleurs,
Et même à nous, auteurs de ces vieilles rubriques,
Réciter en hurlant ses tirades publiques?"

J'aurais pu (mon orgueil aussi haut que les monts
Domine la nuée et le cri des démons)
Détourner simplement ma tête souveraine,
Si je n'eusse pas vu parmi leur troupe obscène,
Crime qui n'a pas fait chanceler le soleil!
La reine de mon cœur au regard nonpareil,
Qui riait avec eux de ma sombre détresse
Et leur versait parfois quelque sale caresse.

BEATRICE

Once in this leafless and ashen landscape,
as I was wandering here and there
lamenting to nature
while grinding my thoughts to a point on my heart,
I saw, in broad daylight,
a great and funereal cloud bear down upon my head.
On it was a troupe of vicious demons
who resembled cruel and curious dwarfs.
Considering me coldly, they looked at each other
like passersby who have marveled at a lunatic.
I heard them laugh and whisper among themselves
while exchanging many knowing signs and winks.

— "Let us consider at our leisure this caricature,
this shadow of a Hamlet, imitating his posture,
his indecisive gaze, his hair in the wind.
Is it not a shame to behold this bon vivant,
this tramp, this actor on vacation, this rogue,
who because he knows how to play his role artfully,
tries to interest the eagles, the crickets,
the rivulets, and the flowers in his song of woe,
and even bellows out to us, the authors
of these old troubles, his tirades."

I might have been able to turn haughtily from them
(for my pride is as high as mountains
and can dominate clouds and the cries of demons),
if I had not seen among their obscene troupe
— O a crime that would not cause the sun to falter! —
the queen of my heart, the one with that unmistakable
look, laughing with them at my somber distress
and giving them, from time to time, a foul caress.

11 Eugène Delacroix
*Hamlet Following the
Ghost of His Father,* 1835

Baudelaire's purpose — to demonstrate his own pain — are quite different, the poet has recognized an analogous sentiment in the painter and exploited it in the complex process of pursuing his own artistic ends.

In "La Béatrice," Baudelaire's suffering is intensified by the notion that he could have ignored the fiends who mocked him were his beloved not among them offering kisses. The theme of painful disillusionment with the ideal is at the center of the poem. He sharpens the bite of this theme by surrounding his lover with Goya's filthy demons and then contrasting her, ironically named after Dante's beatific love, to Delacroix's effete and delicate Hamlet. The poignant tension

in the poem derives from Baudelaire's facility, even if subconscious, for extracting subtle elements from the art of Goya and Delacroix and integrating them into his own. That Dante and Shakespeare are also present testifies to the rich fabric of allusion in Baudelaire's poetry and the ever-present nourishment that the arts supply to one another.

The Baudelaire poem that is most well known for its relationship with the visual arts is "Les Phares" ("Beacons"). Beacons, of course, are guiding lights for voyagers, and "Les Phares" is Baudelaire's tribute in verse to those great painters who have acted as guides through the darkness for

14 Rembrandt van Rijn
Christ with the Sick around Him, Receiving Little Children, 1649

15 Rembrandt van Rijn, *The Three Crosses,* 1653

both ordinary mortals and poets across the ages. They have, as the poem reveals, not only lighted the way for "chasseurs perdus dans les grands bois" ("hunters lost in the great wood"), but served as a chain connecting the lamentations and ecstasies of generations. The art of the painters is, for Baudelaire, the best evidence before God of dignity in a race otherwise wallowing in depravity.

"Les Phares" is a poem that serves as a piece of art criticism. Baudelaire believed that the best and most natural criticism of one art form was a response to it in another. In "Les Phares" he is fulfilling and enlarging upon what he wrote in his "Salon de 1846": "The best account of a picture may well be a sonnet or an elegy."[16] Seeing how the haunting chiaroscuro of two of the greatest etchings ever made merges in Baudelaire's imagery in his stanza on Rembrandt (FIGS. 14, 15), or how Baudelaire captures the dizzying glamour and lunacy in a Watteau *fête galante* in a few quick phrases, brush strokes of his own, as it were, becomes an exercise in understanding how pictures can inspire poems. "Les Phares" also testifies to the diversity of visual art that stirred Baudelaire's poetic imagination — from the pas-

sion of suffering in Michelangelo and Rembrandt to Goya's grotesqueries to Watteau's airy *fêtes*. A stanza of "Les Phares" is not only his poetical/critical commentary on a painter like Rembrandt or Delacroix, but also an analogy in words for a creation in paint, one that simultaneously demonstrates how all of the arts, music included, have the capacity to inspire one another. These relationships among the arts come under the rubric of what Baudelaire called "correspondences" in his famous poem of the same title.

With its mystical and Symbolist ambiguities, "Correspondances" establishes Baudelaire's commitment to the idea that the arts have an underlying unity. In the forests of symbols, he says, the boundaries between art forms dissolve and scents, colors, and sounds correspond to each other. An artist entering this realm can receive inspiration directly from an artist in another medium by means of a lingua franca of the arts. When Baudelaire attended a series of concerts in which he first heard Richard Wagner's "true music," he was transported into a realm where Wagner's ideas could inspire analogous ones in him. As Samuel Cramer, the central character in

CORRESPONDANCES

La Nature est un temple où de vivants piliers
Laissent parfois sortir de confuses paroles;
L'homme y passe à travers des forêts de symboles
Qui l'observent avec des regards familiers.

Comme de longs échos qui de loin se confondent
Dans une ténébreuse et profonde unité,
Vaste comme la nuit et comme la clarté,
Les parfums, les couleurs et les sons se répondent.

Il est des parfums frais comme des chairs d'enfants,
Doux comme les hautbois, verts comme les prairies,
— Et d'autres, corrompus, riches et triomphants,

Ayant l'expansion des choses infinies,
Comme l'ambre, le musc, le benjoin et l'encens,
Qui chantent les transports de l'esprit et des sens.

CORRESPONDENCES

Nature is a temple whose living columns
sometimes allow confused words to escape;
man passes through these forests of symbols,
which regard him with familiar looks.

As diffuse echoes from afar mingle
in a shadowy and profound unison
as vast as the darkness and the light,
scents, colors and sounds commune.

Here are some perfumes fresh as infants' skin,
sweet as the oboe's song and green as the prairies
— while others, corrupt, rich and triumphant,

have the expansiveness of infinite things,
like ambergris, musk, benzoin, and incense,
that chant the ecstasies of the spirit and the senses.

Baudelaire's only short story, "La Fanfarlo," says (describing himself, who is clearly representative of the author), "he was at once all the artists he had known and all the books he had read . . . and was still profoundly original." For Baudelaire, contact with a painting, poem, or piece of music "throws open immense vistas to the most adventurous imaginations."[17] Baudelaire termed the ability of an artist to appropriate that which is poetic "naïveté," by which he meant an uncalculated reception of an aspect of another work of art. Baudelaire thought that poetry must come into a painting without the artist's knowledge. It is in this spirit of Baudelairean naïveté that Jean Prévost could observe, "Delacroix helped Baudelaire to know himself and to dare to dream his dreams."[18] For Baudelaire, "The arts aspire, if not to complement one another, at least to lend one another new energies."[19]

Baudelaire modestly called himself "a man who, though lacking vast knowledge, has the love of painting to the tips of his very nerves."[20] With this spiritual and visceral connection to painting, it is not surprising that Baudelaire found in it "new energies" for his poems, or that his poetry, so in harmony with and compelled by painting, should speak to generations of painters. Images derived from Delacroix, Michelangelo, Goya, and others are woven throughout the fabric of Baudelaire's poetry, confirming the intimacy of "the sister arts," an intimacy that blossomed even further in the relationship between his poetry and the art of his contemporaries Honoré Daumier, Charles Méryon, and Edouard Manet and that continues to be revealed in the work of those who followed: Paul Gauguin, Edvard Munch, Odilon Redon, Auguste Rodin, Henri Matisse, Georges Rouault, René Magritte, William Baziotes, Robert Motherwell, and many others. That the artists named here are so revered testifies both to Baudelaire's acuity as an observer of art and to the power of his poetry to inspire it.

16 Gustave Courbet
The Painter's Studio,
A Real Allegory, 1855

Baudelaire, reading, is seated at the far right. Courbet's rendering of the poet in his allegorical studio derives from his portrait of Baudelaire from 1847 (**FRONTISPIECE**)

17 Eugène Delacroix, *Dante and Virgil*, 1822

Delacroix, lac de sang hanté des mauvais anges,
Ombragé par un bois de sapins toujours vert,
Où, sous un ciel chagrin, des fanfares étranges
Passent, comme un soupir étouffé de Weber.

From "Les Phares"

Delacroix — lake of blood haunted by evil angels,
darkly shadowed by a forest forever green,
where under a despairing sky strange fanfares
pass like a muffled sigh from Weber.

From "Beacons"

Voyage into the Depths

When Baudelaire was twelve, he had intimations of an inner struggle in which evil was a combatant, but he was not yet convinced that evil controlled him. From school he wrote to his mother and stepfather, "You've despaired of me as one would despair of a son whose evil was beyond cure, to whom everything was indifferent . . . who was weak, cowardly, lazy and lacked the courage to pull himself together. I have been weak, cowardly, lazy. . . . But as nothing can alter the heart, my heart, which for all its faults has its good points, has remained unaffected."[1] Twenty years later his tune had changed. He wrote to his mother in 1854, "I believe that my life has been damned from the very beginning and that it is damned for eternity."[2] In the earlier letter he reveals the roots of his lifelong pain, his consciousness that his evil might be incurable and might be perceived as such by his mother. In the later letter he has converted his doubt into certainty. And he did not believe this just for himself. Life itself was an inevitable voyage into the depths guaranteed not only to result in excruciating remorse over sins committed, but also to be attended by constant despair, what Baudelaire called "spleen." Spleen derived from a paradox at the center of Baudelaire's existence. The self-directed voyage downward was accompanied by a persistent yearning to rise to the ideal. The problem was in the mind. Human beings were capable of knowing the nature of both spiritual harmony and grace while at the same time understanding full well that they were unable to attain them. The especially keen and sensitive mind, the mind of the poet, was fated to suffer even more exquisitely than others because his perception of beauty and his temptation for the corrupt were most intense. These contradictions permeate Baudelaire's poetry.

Baudelaire was a child of the Romantic epoch but became an adult in an age rebelling against Romanticism. The Romantic quest of the early part of the century had dissipated. Both the bright side of Romanticism, the search for liberty, equality, and the brotherhood of man, for a utopia based on the efflorescence of the human spirit, and its darker side, with its Gothic and satanic permutations, had given way to a solid reliance on the real, on science, and on material progress. By 1850 it was not fashionable either among thinkers or within popular culture to be a serious believer in evil or the depravity of man. Among nationalists, realists, Darwinists, positivists, and incipient Marxists, the nineteenth century left little room for those who confessed serious belief in the existence of evil in human nature. They were considered atavistic, eccentric, or decadent. But Baudelaire, though certainly eccentric and fascinated by the decadent, like Dostoyevski, was very serious and clear-eyed about his notion of the existence of evil in human nature. His "flowers of evil" are, in a sense, his "notes from underground."[3] He was not a poet who wished to celebrate the decadent or appeal to such tastes in others. As mentioned earlier, when Flaubert suggested to him that he "insisted too much on the spirit of evil," he replied not only that he could account for human behavior in no other way, but also that he was aware of being in opposition to "the entire confederated nineteenth century." Baudelaire was not a decadent writer in the common sense of the word but a realist who understood that what was real was more than what met the eye. He was not the kind of realist who wanted to present an unvarnished account of the sordidness of Parisian life. He was a muckraker of a different sort, one who dug relentlessly through

AU LECTEUR

La sottise, l'erreur, le péché, la lésine,
Occupent nos esprits et travaillent nos corps,
Et nous alimentons nos aimables remords,
Comme les mendiants nourrissent leur vermine.

Nos péchés sont têtus, nos repentirs sont lâches;
Nous nous faisons payer grassement nos aveux,
Et nous rentrons gaiement dans le chemin bourbeux,
Croyant par de vils pleurs laver toutes nos taches.

Sur l'oreiller du mal c'est Satan Trismégiste
Qui berce longuement notre esprit enchanté,
Et le riche métal de notre volonté
Est tout vaporisé par ce savant chimiste.

C'est le Diable qui tient les fils qui nous remuent!
Aux objets répugnants nous trouvons des appas;
Chaque jour vers l'Enfer nous descendons d'un pas,
Sans horreur, à travers des ténèbres qui puent.

Ainsi qu'un débauché pauvre qui baise et mange
Le sein martyrisé d'une antique catin,
Nous volons au passage un plaisir clandestin
Que nous pressons bien fort comme une vieille orange.

Serré, fourmillant, comme un million d'helminthes,
Dans nos cerveaux ribote un peuple de Démons,
Et, quand nous respirons, la Mort dans nos poumons
Descend, fleuve invisible, avec de sourdes plaintes.

Si le viol, le poison, le poignard, l'incendie,
N'ont pas encor brodé de leurs plaisants dessins
Le canevas banal de nos piteux destins,
C'est que notre âme, hélas! n'est pas assez hardie.

Mais parmi les chacals, les panthères, les lices,
Les singes, les scorpions, les vautours, les serpents,
Les monstres glapissants, hurlants, grognants,
        rampants,
Dans la ménagerie infâme de nos vices,

Il en est un plus laid, plus méchant, plus immonde!
Quoiqu'il ne pousse ni grands gestes ni grands cris,
Il ferait volontiers de la terre un débris
Et dans un bâillement avalerait le monde;

C'est l'Ennui! — l'œil chargé d'un pleur involontaire,
Il rêve d'échafauds en fumant son houka.
Tu le connais, lecteur, ce monstre délicat,
— Hypocrite lecteur, — mon semblable, — mon frère!

TO THE READER

Stupidity, iniquity, sin, and avarice
occupy our souls and work over our bodies,
and we feed our amiable remorse
as beggars nourish their vermin.

Our sins are unyielding, our repentances cowardly;
we make ourselves pay roundly in our confessions
and then return happily to the mire, believing we have
washed away the stains with our vile tears.

On a bed of evil Thrice Magisterial Satan
endlessly rocks our enchanted spirit
until the rich metal of our will
is vaporized by this shrewd alchemist.

It is the Devil who pulls the strings that move us!
In the repugnant we find charm, and
each day we descend another step toward Hell,
without horror, through the putrid shadows.

Like some poor debauchee who kisses and eats
at the martyred breast of an ancient whore,
along the way we steal clandestine pleasures,
squeezing them dry like an old orange.

Packed tightly and swarming like maggots,
a mob of Demons makes merry in our brains,
and when we breathe, Death descends into our lungs,
an invisible river with unheard moans.

If rape, poison, the dagger, arson,
have not yet embroidered their agreeable patterns
on the banal canvas of our sorry fate,
it is only because our soul, alas, is not daring enough.

But here among the jackals, panthers, mongrels,
apes, the scorpions, vultures, snakes,
the monsters that squeal, scream, and groan
in the infamous menagerie of our vices,

there is one uglier, more wicked, and more filthy than
the rest. Though he makes no grand gestures or loud
cries, he would gladly turn the earth into a wasteland
and in a yawn swallow the world.

It is Ennui! Eye filled with involuntary tears,
he dreams of scaffolds while smoking his hookah.
You know him, reader, this delicate monster
— hypocrite reader — my fellow man — my brother!

18 Francisco Goya
Where Is Mother Going?,
1799

the mud because he knew one of its main components was human tears. He was a traveler in the darker quarters because they were an inescapably real portion of life's lot. His goal was a confrontation with the dark side of existence. His fate as a human being drove him downward, and his role as poet compelled him to crystallize the experience in his art.

Satanic Images: Goya, Delacroix

Literal satanism and evil are also difficult for the twentieth-century mind to accept. This is so despite the fact that the chaotic and perverse behavior of human beings has been broadcast more widely and more consistently during this epoch than any other. Baudelaire's poetry is rooted in awareness of this disorder. He saw it at the center of the human soul. What his contemporaries often characterized as his desire to scandalize and shock his readers is based on his need to reveal the content of that soul. Although many have been attracted to the scandalous side of his life and work, even used him as a standard by which to measure devotion to debauchery, the macabre, misogyny, and decadence in general, he has been so highly valued in this century because of his ability to recast the struggle between good and evil as a modern allegory. Moreover, he attracts the modern sensibility because his setting is the city and because the underpinning of his allegory is not black magic but a poetic evocation of obsessive guilt. Modern readers are on familiar territory when they accompany Baudelaire on his voyage into the depths.

In "Au Lecteur" ("To the Reader"), the prefatory poem to *Les Fleurs du mal,* Baudelaire demands that the reader, his hypocritical twin, acknowledge the truth. Human beings are imbued with sin and vice; yet they comfortably forgive themselves. The devil has convinced everyone that he doesn't exist — one of his clev-

65.

Donde vá mamá?

19 Eugène Delacroix
Mephistopheles Flying,
c. 1828

erest tricks, according to the poet. Baudelaire characterizes man as plain cloth on whom temptation is embroidered. These embroideries, bound up as they are with the stuff of being, irresistibly draw men toward the devil and into the depths. That Baudelaire should use such a metaphor is a clue to the origins of many of the images in the poem. They derive from visual art. When he writes "C'est le Diable qui tient les fils qui nous remuent!" ("It is the Devil who pulls the strings that move us!"), Satan is a malevolent puppeteer who hovers above rather than residing below, recalling the fiendish creatures coursing through the skies in works by Goya and Delacroix.

Baudelaire was undoubtedly inspired by Goya's fiends (FIGS. 12, 13, 18), not merely because they were bizarre, but also because "all those distortions, those bestial faces, those diabolic grimaces of his [Goya's] are impregnated with humanity."[4] Well before the *Caprichos* had stirred Baudelaire, they had also fascinated Delacroix. He had studied them as far back as 1820 and undoubtedly drew on them in 1825, when a dramatic adaptation of Goethe's *Faust* inspired him to produce a set of lithographs for a French edition of *Faust*. They were so masterful that, upon seeing some of them, Goethe himself said, "I must confess that M. Delacroix has, in some scenes, surpassed my own notions."[5]

Baudelaire could not have helped being affected by them as well. Delacroix's Mephistopheles is in flight above the landscape (FIG. 19). With the setting sun in the background and the blackness of night in the foreground, the power of the devil to "pull the strings that move us" is manifest. Delacroix's figure irresistibly tempts humanity to follow and must have appealed to Baudelaire's sense of evil as "external to man." At the same time, along with Goya's groups of demons, such a picture functions as a metaphor for his profound sense of evil as internal and virtually organic because "Dans nos cerveaux ribote un peuple de Démons" ("a mob of Demons makes merry in our brains"). Baudelaire's belief that twilight is the most vulnerable time for human beings in their struggle with their own nature is also reinforced by Delacroix's lithograph, which may have inspired the passage in his poem "Le Crépuscule du soir" ("Evening Twilight") that claims dusk is the time when "l'homme impatient se change en bête fauve" ("impatient man changes into a wild beast") and when "des démons malsains dans l'atmosphère / S'éveillent lourdement" ("unhealthy demons rise heavily into the atmosphere"). A Satan very much akin to Delacroix's also appears in "L'Imprévu" ("The Unforeseen"), where he commands, " 'Reconnaissez Satan à son rire vainqueur, / Enorme et laid comme le monde!' " ("Recognize Satan with his conquering laugh, enormous and ugly as the world!") and then informs his human quarry, " 'Je vais vous emporter à travers l'épaisseur, / Compagnons de ma triste joie' " (" 'I am going to carry you down into the depths, companions of my sad joy' "). Delacroix and Baudelaire shared the Romantic obsession with the duality of good and evil inherent in the human condition and illustrated it in their respective pictures of Satan rising from the depths, asserting his strength and exerting control over a vulnerable humanity. Their sentiments as well as their images correspond. Goethe's observation about Delacroix's response to *Faust* could just as easily apply to Baudelaire: "*Faust* is a work which passes from heaven to earth, from the possible to the impossible, from the gross to the exquisite; all the antitheses which the play of bold imagination can create are there brought together; this is why Monsieur Delacroix felt at home in it."[6]

Satan is such a compelling character to Baudelaire because his origins are in the divine, yet he has fallen and taken up residence in the depths. The poet wrote in his diary, "There are in every

20 James Ensor, *Salon des Cents (Self-Portrait with Demons),* 1898

man, at every hour, two simultaneous allegiances, one to God, the other to Satan," and added, "Invocation of God, or spirituality, is a desire to climb higher; that of Satan, or animality, is joy in descent" (1:682–683). The lines in "Au Lecteur," "Chaque jour vers l'Enfer nous descendons d'un pas, / Sans horreur, à travers des ténèbres qui puent" ("Each day we descend another step toward Hell, without horror, through the putrid shadows"), emerge from this perverse joy in descent. Moreover, they conjure the image of the staircase as the designated means for the downward journey. In the poem "Sur *Le Tasse en Prison* d'Eugène Delacroix" ("On *Tasso in Prison* by Eugène Delacroix") Baudelaire contemplates Delacroix's picture of Tasso in his cell as he "Mesure d'un regard que la terreur enflamme / L'escalier de vertige où s'abîme son âme" ("Measures with a gaze inflamed by terror the dizzying staircase where his soul is sinking").[7]

Images of Darkness: Piranesi, Redon, Delacroix

The prototypical images in visual art of stairways, especially ones leading down into prisons, are those in the etchings of Giovanni Battista Piranesi (1720–1778). Over and over Piranesi depicted monumental staircases descending into cavernous, subterranean chambers, and over and over stairways leading to and from Hell appear in *Les Fleurs du mal*. Although there is no specific mention of Piranesi in Baudelaire's writings, the influence is distinct. As Georges Poulet notes, "The itinerary followed by the damned in Baudelaire's writings is essentially Piranesian," and "Piranesi's world and Baudelaire's world are alike. Each throws light on the other so much so that the latter comes to seem like a verbal commentary on the former."[8] Both have described the world of the abyss, or, better, the world as abyss. The prison interiors in Piranesi's *Carceri* etchings (FIG. 21) must

21 Giovanni Piranesi
*The Staircase with
Trophies,* 1761

22 Eugène Delacroix, *The Death of Sardanapalus*, c. 1827

have arisen in Baudelaire's brain as what he elsewhere described as "dreams of terraces, towers, ramparts, rising to unknown heights and plunging to immense depths."[9] With their torture racks and smoking fires, they could be as easily taken for portraits of Hell or the unconscious mind as for Roman jails. They are the visual equivalent, if not the source, for the picture Baudelaire drew in his poem "L'Irrémédiable," where he symbolizes the voyage through life as a descent on a treacherous stairway, "Un damné descendant sans lampe, / Au bord d'un gouffre dont l'odeur / Trahit l'humide profondeur, / D'éternels escaliers sans rampe" ("A damned one descending without a lamp next to an abyss the odor of which betrays its damp depths, on eternal stairways without a rail"). For Baudelaire, Hell's stairway goes up as well as down. Mortals descend but devils rise. He begins the prose poem "Les Tentations" ("The Temptations")[10] with a passage that suggests that it was inspired by another Delacroix lithograph from the *Faust* series (FIG. 23 and accompanying text from poem). Here Baudelaire has assembled, in his usual fashion, visual images from various sources to serve his own purposes. In "Les Tentations" the poet has induced Goethe's devils, as pictured by Delacroix, to climb Piranesi's staircase.

Just as Piranesian images inspired Baudelairean ones, so Baudelaire's poetic expression of the voyage into the depths had a resonance for painters who scrutinized their inner selves and shared something of Baudelaire's dualistic view of human nature. The intimate relationship between the individual and evil as it emerges in "Au Lecteur" and many other poems in *Les Fleurs du mal* is given graphic immediacy by the work of Odilon Redon (1840–1916). Redon belonged to the generation that followed Baudelaire and worked in Paris within the milieu of *l'Esprit Décadent* (the Decadent Spirit) and Symbolism in the 1880s, but, like

23 Eugène Delacroix
Faust Courting Margarete,
c. 1828

Deux superbes Satans et une Diablesse, non moins extraordinaire, ont la nuit dernière monté l'escalier mystérieux par où l'Enfer donne assaut à la faiblesse de l'homme qui dort, et communique en secret avec lui. Et ils sont venus se poser glorieusement devant moi, debout comme sur une estrade. Une splendeur sulfureuse émanait de ces trois personnages, qui se détachaient ainsi du fond opaque de la nuit. Ils avaient l'air si fier et si plein de domination, que je les pris d'abord tous les trois pour de vrais Dieux.

From "Les Tentations ou Eros, Plutus et la gloire"

Last night, two superb Satans and a no less extraordinary she-devil climbed that mysterious staircase by which the powers of Hell assault the vulnerability of sleeping humanity and communicate with them in secret. They came and gloriously posed themselves before me, as if on a dais. A sulfurous splendor emanated from these three personages, highlighting them against the opaque depths of the night. They had an air about them so proud and so overpowering that at first I took all three for true Gods.

From "The Temptations, or Eros, Pluto and Fame"

24 Odilon Redon
On the Dish, 1879

La tête, avec l'amas de sa crinière sombre
    Et de ses bijoux précieux,

Sur la table de nuit, comme une renoncule,
    Repose; et, vide de pensers,
Un regard vague et blanc comme le crépuscule
    S'échappe des yeux révulsés.

          From "Une Martyre"

The head, with its somber mane and precious jewels,

reposes on the night table like a ranunculus;
    and empty of all thought,
a look, vague and blank as the twilight,
    escapes from the rolled-back eyes.

          From "A Martyr"

Baudelaire, he was a highly individualistic creator whose art eluded the confines of any particular movement. Also, the often bizarre and macabre content of his work, like Baudelaire's, reflected a need to express his innermost vision and not a desire to exploit the sensational.

During Redon's lifetime the writer of decadent fiction and art critic Joris-Karl Huysmans (1848–1907) claimed that Redon was the direct descendant of Edgar Allan Poe and Baudelaire. He characterized Redon's art as "a veritable transformation of one art into another."[11] In Huysmans's decadent novel *A Rebours* the hero des Esseintes reads *Les Fleurs du mal* with its "ideal of sickly deprivation"[12] and decorates his chamber with Redon's drawings, which "passed all bounds, transgressing in a thousand ways the established laws of pictorial art, utterly fantastic and revolutionary, the work of a mad and morbid genius."[13] In his *Homage to Redon* poet and critic Gabriel Sarrazin also compares Redon to Poe and Baudelaire. He says that when he visited the painter's studio, he found a strong correspondence between Redon's work and "the two poets of whom we spoke constantly at that time."[14] Similar comments have continued through the present. Art historian John Rewald asks, "How could he [Redon] not discover in Poe's texts, translated by Baudelaire, innumerable somber images akin to his own dreams; and above all, how could he resist the ardent rhythms, the melodious verse of Baudelaire, poetic equivalent of Delacroix's paintings?" Rewald continues, "In Baudelaire's poems, Redon found expressed a peculiar 'spleen,' a predilection for the macabre which struck a chord in his own soul."[15]

The connection that Rewald suggests among Delacroix, Baudelaire, and Redon is particularly interesting because it is not restricted to just general poetic qualities that all three artists possess. It speaks to their common interest in the dark side

SPLEEN

Je suis comme le roi d'un pays pluvieux,
Riche, mais impuissant, jeune et pourtant très-vieux,
Qui, de ses précepteurs méprisant les courbettes,
S'ennuie avec ses chiens comme avec d'autres bêtes.
Rien ne peut l'égayer, ni gibier, ni faucon,
Ni son peuple mourant en face du balcon.
Du bouffon favori la grotesque ballade
Ne distrait plus le front de ce cruel malade;
Son lit fleurdelisé se transforme en tombeau,
Et les dames d'atour, pour qui tout prince est beau,
Ne savent plus trouver d'impudique toilette
Pour tirer un souris de ce jeune squelette.
Le savant qui lui fait de l'or n'a jamais pu
De son être extirper l'élément corrompu,
Et dans ces bains de sang qui des Romains nous
       viennent,
Et dont sur leurs vieux jours les puissants se
       souviennent,
Il n'a su réchauffer ce cadavre hébété
Où coule au lieu de sang l'eau verte du Léthé.

SPLEEN

I am like the king of a rainy country,
rich but impotent, young yet somehow very old,
who, scorning his obsequious tutors,
bores himself with his dogs and other beasts.
Nothing can amuse him, not his game animals, not his
falcons, not even his people dying before his balcony.
No longer can this cruel sufferer be distracted
by his favorite clown's grotesque ballads.
His royal bed is become a tomb, and the
women in their turn, for whom every king is beautiful,
can find no new shameless costumes
to make this young skeleton smile.
The alchemist who makes gold for him has never been able
to extract the corrupt element from his being;
and even these blood baths, which the Romans gave us,

and which in their old age the powerful will recall,

cannot reinflame his cadaverous body,
where in place of blood flow the waters of Lethe.

of human nature and leads to an image that can be traced from Delacroix, the grand Romantic of the first half of the century, to Redon, the delicate and fantastic Symbolist of the second, and that passes through Baudelaire, the poet who was both. Jean Prévost, in his well-known study of Baudelaire's poetic sources, points out that the image of the decapitated woman in Baudelaire's poem "Une Martyre," an image of a woman lying on a bed in a sumptuous chamber, beheaded by her deviant lover, has its roots in Delacroix's monumental painting *The Death of Sardanapalus* (FIG. 22).[16] Partly inspired by a tragedy by Byron, Delacroix pictures Sardanapalus, the last king of Assyria, on a combination bed and funeral pyre. He gazes out over his assembled subjects as they carry out his orders to slaughter his horses and his concubines before he immolates them along with himself. He evidently wishes to reserve the sadistic pleasure of such carnage for his own eyes before he is overwhelmed by his enemies. According to Prévost, Delacroix kept a sketch of this painting for himself in which the head of the nude figure on the bed is actually severed. Baudelaire saw this sketch on a visit to Delacroix's studio and adapted the image for "Une Martyre." Moreover, critic Anita Brookner is convinced that Delacroix's painting made such an overwhelming impression on Baudelaire that he turned it, "slightly symbolized," into one of his great "Spleen" poems (PAGE 53).[17]

In "Une Martyre" the retinue has been vastly reduced from the host of martyrs in Delacroix's painting to a single figure, but both works exude an atmosphere of luxuriant horror, as does the "Spleen" poem. In his essays Baudelaire often emphasized Delacroix's "slaughtered victims [and] ravished women," remarking that "there was much of the *savage* in Eugène Delacroix — this was in fact the most precious part of his soul, the part which was entirely dedicated to the painting of his dreams and to the worship of his art."[18] On seeing *The Death of Sardanapalus* on exhibition in 1862, long after he had seen it the first time and years after he had written the poems, he noted, "Many times my dreams have been filled with the magnificent forms that stir in this vast picture, itself marvelous as a dream" (2:733–734). Baudelaire cherished this taste for the grotesque and confessed that he was sorry for the poet who could not understand it. Such a poet, he wrote, "is a harp that lacks a base string" (1:549). Baudelaire's affinity for the horrifying in art was not just a self-indulgent preference for the grotesque, but a necessary means of achieving the most encompassing perspective on life as he saw it. Delacroix's works, he wrote, "contain nothing but devastation, massacres, conflagrations; everything bears witness against the eternal and incorrigible barbarity of man."[19] What Baudelaire imagined to be the precious savagery of Delacroix's dreams fed his own.

And Baudelaire's dreams fed Redon's, as evidenced by his first and perhaps greatest album of prints, *Dans le rêve (In the Dream)*. Redon was steeped in Baudelaire. He not only knew his poetry, but also had read many of his letters, which were published in the *Mercure de France,* as well as his critical essays and early biographical accounts.[20] It is not unlikely that the title of Redon's album derived from Baudelaire's poem "La Voix," in which he wrote, " 'viens voyager dans les rêves / Au-delà du possible, au-delà du connu!' " (" 'come voyage in dreams, beyond the possible, beyond the known!' "), not only because Baudelaire's lines include "dans les rêves" but because Baudelaire's sentiment is so in tune with

Redon's ideal. Redon believed that an artist should transmit the impressions experienced in his dreams to his audience by putting "the logic of the visible in the service of the invisible."[21]

In *Dans le rêve* is a lithograph entitled *Sur la coupe (On the Dish)* (FIG. 24). It is a picture of a severed head on a pedestal or small table. The diminutive, spare scene of Redon's lithograph is a far cry from the ghastly slaughter of Delacroix's grand painting, but it is very close to the one pictured in Baudelaire's poem — the head on the table with its "vague and blank" stare and its "rolled-back eyes." Redon was not, however, illustrating Baudelaire's poem so much as creating an image of his own to fulfill his own artistic intent, borrowing from Baudelaire in the process. He did, in fact, draw heads unencumbered by bodies in a number of works, including one illustrating a poem in *Les Fleurs du mal*. But the striking correspondence of features in this case suggests that Baudelaire's image worked its way from "Une Martyre" into Redon's picture, just as Delacroix's image did into Baudelaire's poem.[22]

In 1890 Redon created nine drawings to accompany poems from *Les Fleurs du mal*. Each drawing bears a line from one of the poems as its legend. "Sans cesse à mes côtés s'agite le Démon" ("Ceaselessly the devil stirs at my side") (FIG. 25) from the poem "La Destruction" harks back to the intimate relationship between Satan and humans rendered in "Au Lecteur." The destructive power of evil is particularly insidious in "La Destruction" because it recognizes and plays upon the poet's love of art and beauty. Baudelaire acknowledges that evil, "sachant [son] grand amour de l'Art" ("knowing [his] great love of Art"), takes the form of "la plus séduisante des femmes" ("the most seductive of women"), thus suggesting the connection in his mind between the effect on him of a beautiful woman and of art. In the sonnet, the speaker laments that the devil keeps him

25 Odilon Redon
Ceaselessly the Devil Stirs at My Side, 1890

hidden from God's regard, "Haletant et brisé de fatigue, au milieu / Des plaines de l'Ennui, profondes et désertes" ("gasping and broken by fatigue, in the middle of the plains of Ennui, deep and deserted"). In the picture, the devil, in the form of a woman, is close by the side of another figure (the poet or the painter?) seated on a rocky prominence in the midst of the sea. Hidden from the view of both demon and person, an enormous sun sets on the horizon. Redon has used the sun as a metaphor for God's face and created a massive boulder as the means of separating the devil's victim from God. For the barren plains of Ennui, he has substituted the sea. Redon's inspirations, like Baudelaire's, came from many sources, and "La Destruction" may not have been the only poem from *Les Fleurs du mal* he drew on for this image. Baudelaire created other versions of the abyss that may also have had an effect. In "De profundis clamavi," he writes, "C'est un univers morne à l'horizon plombé / Où nagent dans la nuit l'horreur et le blasphème; / Un soleil sans chaleur plane au-dessus six mois, / Et les six autres mois la nuit couvre la terre" ("It is a dismal universe with a horizon of lead where horror and blasphemy swim in the night; half the year a sun without heat hovers above; the other half, night covers the earth"). Another drawing Redon included in his *Fleurs du mal* series is based on the poem "Le Gouffre" ("The Abyss"). The lines he chose for its legend, "Sur le fond de mes nuits Dieu de son doigt savant / Dessine un cauchemar multiforme et sans trêve" ("On the depth of my nights, God with his clever finger draws a ceaseless, multiform nightmare"), signify Redon's clear understanding of Baudelaire's attitude toward the forces of darkness.

Beauty: Women and the Depths

A form of solace that Baudelaire constantly sought in life was beauty. In fact, he finally identified an

26 Ernest Christophe
*La Comédie humaine
(Le Masque),* 1876

— Mais non! ce n'est qu'un masque, un décor
    suborneur,
Ce visage éclairé d'une exquise grimace,
Et, regarde, voici, crispée atrocement,
La véritable tête, et la sincère face
Renversée à l'abri de la face qui ment.
Pauvre grande beauté! la magnifique fleuve
De tes pleurs aboutit dans mon cœur soucieux;
Ton mensonge m'enivre, et mon âme s'abreuve
Aux flots que la Douleur fait jaillir de tes yeux!

— Mais pourquoi pleure-t-elle? Elle, beauté parfaite
Qui mettrait à ses pieds le genre humain vaincu,
Quel mal mystérieux ronge son flanc d'athlète?

— Elle pleure, insensé, parce qu'elle a vécu!
Et parce qu'elle vit! Mais ce qu'elle déplore
Surtout, ce qui la fait frémir jusqu'aux genoux,
C'est que demain, hélas! il faudra vivre encore!
Demain, après-demain et toujours!—comme nous!

From "Le Masque"

— But no! This is only a mask, a seductive cover
over this face enlightened in exquisite grimace;
and look, here, terribly strained,
is the true head, and the sincere face
is hidden in the shadow of the face that lies.
Wretched and great beauty! The magnificent stream
of your tears flows into my caring heart;
your lie intoxicates me, and my soul quenches
its thirst in the flow of grief that gushes from your eyes.

— But why does she weep? She, perfect beauty
who could have conquered all mankind,
what mysterious evil gnaws at her lithe flank?

— She weeps, you innocent, because she has lived
and because she lives now. But what she deplores,
what makes her tremble down to her knees
is that tomorrow, alas, she must continue to live.
Tomorrow, the day after and always! — like us!

From "The Mask"

inescapable morality in its pursuit. And for him the perverse irony was that the upward course followed in that pursuit inevitably resulted in a plunge into the depths — not just for him personally, he felt, but for all true artists and poets.

Baudelaire defined beauty a number of times and in a variety of ways within his critical writings. A consistent concept, however, persists throughout, and it is not at all surprising that, like so many other concepts of his, it bears the stamp of duality. In the chapter entitled "On the Heroism of Modern Life" from the essay "Salon de 1846," written near the beginning of his life as a critic, he states, "All forms of beauty, like all possible phenomena, contain an element of the eternal and an element of the transitory — of the absolute and of the particular."[23] Near the beginning of his essay "Le Peintre de la vie moderne" ("The Painter of Modern Life"), which was written close to the end of his life as a critic, he elaborates: "Beauty is made up of an eternal, invariable element, whose quantity it is excessively difficult to determine, and of a relative, circumstantial element, which will be if you like, whether severally or all at once, the age, its fashions, its morals, its emotions. Without this second element, which might be described as the amusing, enticing, appetizing icing on the divine cake, the first element would be beyond our powers of digestion or appreciation, neither adapted nor suitable to human nature. I defy anyone to point to a single scrap of beauty which does not contain these two elements."[24]

These critical formulations have a very different character from the qualities he associates with beauty in his poetry and in his diaries. There he distinguishes between "*the* definition of beauty" and "*my* beauty" (italics mine). His personal beauty "is something intense and sad, something a little vague, leaving scope for conjecture. . . . I mean that a woman's head makes one dream, but in a confused manner, of both pleasure and sadness; it conveys an idea of melancholy, of lassitude, even of satiety — it is a contradictory impression, that is to say, one of ardor and a desire to live associated with a bitterness flowing back from them as if from a sense of deprivation or hopelessness. Mystery and regret are also characteristics of the Beautiful." He continues: "I do not pretend that Joy cannot associate with Beauty, but I will say that Joy is one of her most vulgar adornments, while Melancholy may be called her illustrious companion — to the point that I can scarcely conceive (is my brain become a bewitched mirror?) a type of Beauty in which there is not some sorrow" (1:657–658).

Baudelaire's critical definitions of beauty assume that attainment of beauty is not only desired, but also completely positive. When an artist achieves the proper mix of ingredients, he will accomplish what the critic requires. Although the concept has a dual character, it is a duality of past and present, of absolute and relative, not of good and evil, happiness and despair, life and death. His personal beauty, on the other hand, has paradox built into its very definition. It cannot be achieved without evoking the darker side of life, the side human beings characteristically seek to avoid. This is the poet's beauty, the artist's beauty, what in Delacroix is "the most remarkable quality of all, and that which makes him the true painter of the nineteenth century; it is the unique and persistent melancholy with which all his works are imbued."[25] It is what makes him the "poet-painter."

In the poem "Le Masque" Baudelaire relates his shocking discovery of the link between beauty and sadness in a woman. The poet comes across a statue of an extraordinarily beautiful woman whose anguished face is hidden behind a mask of unblemished delight. The poet is perplexed in the extreme. He asks, "— Mais pourquoi pleure-t-elle? Elle, beauté parfaite / Qui mettrait à ses pieds le genre humain vaincu, / Quel mal mystérieux ronge son flanc d'athlète?" ("— But why does she weep? She, perfect beauty who could have conquered all mankind, what mysterious evil gnaws at her lithe flank?") A second voice in the poem answers the poet: "— Elle pleure, insensé, parce qu'elle a vécu! / Et parce qu'elle vit! Mais ce qu'elle déplore / Surtout, ce qui la fait frémir jusqu'aux genoux, / C'est que demain, hélas! il faudra vivre encore! / Demain, aprés-demain et toujours! — comme nous!" ("— She weeps, you innocent, because she has lived and because she lives now. But what she deplores, what makes her tremble down to her knees is that tomorrow, alas, she must continue to live. Tomorrow, the day after and always! — like us!") Baudelaire's inspiration for this poem was a sculpture by his friend Ernest Christophe (1827–1892) (FIG. 26). At the time Baudelaire first saw the statue, in 1859, Christophe's title for it was La Comédie humaine. In his commentary on this statue in his salon essay for 1859 Baudelaire calls the face that the spectator sees first "a conventional head." "But," he continues, "if you take a further step to the right or the left, you will discover the secret of the allegory, the moral of the fable — the real head, I mean, twisted out of position and in a swoon of agony and tears. What at first had enchanted your eyes was but a mask — the universal mask, your mask, my mask, the pretty fan which a clever hand uses to conceal its pain or remorse from the eyes of the world."[26] Baudelaire dedicated "Le Masque" to Christophe, and it appeared in the 1861 edition of Les Fleurs du mal. Fifteen years later, a decade after Baudelaire's death, Christophe created a monumentally sized version of his sculpture and when he entered it in the Salon of 1876 he changed the title from La Comédie humaine to that of Baudelaire's poem, in homage to the poet. The statue received a medal at the salon and was

purchased by the state and installed in the Tuileries Gardens, where it stood until recently.[27]

In "Hymne à la Beauté" ("Hymn to Beauty"), Baudelaire continues to explore the duality at the heart of beauty: "Viens-tu du ciel profond ou sors-tu de l'abîme, / O Beauté? ton regard, infernal et divin, / Verse confusément le bienfait et le crime" ("Do you come from the depths of the sky or from the abyss, O Beauty? Your look, infernal and divine, pours out a confusion of kindness and crime"). In the prose poem "Le Désir de peindre" ("The Desire to Paint"), he expresses the desire to paint a woman because, although mankind suf-

fers, the artist who is compelled by the desire to paint beauty, in spite of its complex duality, may somehow find relief.

Elle est belle, et plus que belle; elle est surprenante. En elle le noir abonde: et tout ce qu'elle inspire est nocturne et profond. Ses yeux sont deux antres où scintille vaguement le mystère, et son regard illumine comme l'éclair: c'est une explosion dans les ténèbres.

Je la comparerais à un soleil noir, si l'on pouvait concevoir un astre noir versant la lumière et le bonheur.

She is beautiful, more than beautiful; she is

27 Edouard Manet
Jeanne Duval (Baudelaire's Mistress Reclining), 1862

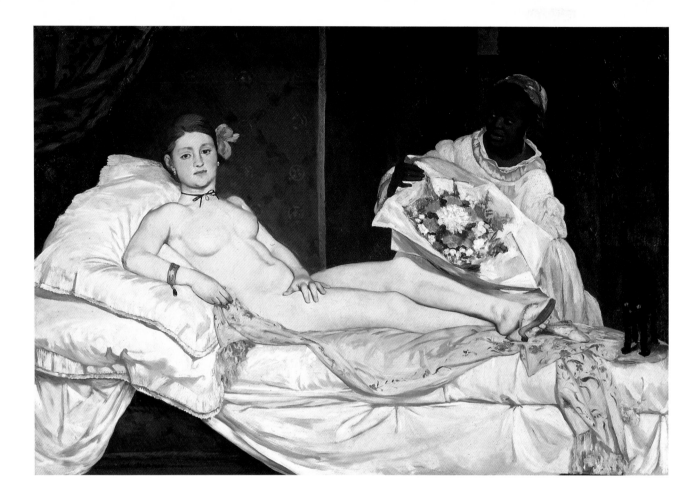

29 Edouard Manet
Olympia, 1863

her creator; the closer the poet or artist comes to achieving beauty, the more certain is his destruction; soaring toward the heights inevitably results in a plunge into the depths. Instead of the fatal black suns of Melencolia's eyes, Beauty's eyes are pure mirrors, but the results are the same: destruction for those who seek out that beauty. And here, too, the woman's victims apparently pursue the privilege of dying under her gaze.

"Les Bijoux" ("Jewels"), one of the poems condemned by the French court shortly after *Les Fleurs du mal* was published in 1857, also turns on the beauty of the temptress who seduces both body and soul. The poet describes a woman dressed only in her jewels as she lies on her couch, striking various poses to arouse him. Danger and pleasure are again linked as she thrusts herself forward "plus câlins que les Anges du mal" ("more tempting than the evil Angels"). The effect of this seductiveness is "troubler le repos où mon âme était mise, / Et pour la déranger du rocher de cristal / Où, calme et solitaire, elle s'était assise'' (''to trouble the repose where my soul resided and extract it from the crystalline rock where, calm and solitary, it was seated''). Here the seductress is the flesh-and-blood version of the dream in stone of ''La Beauté.'' In this poem, however, the stone represents the place of the poet's repose and safety, and it is the seductiveness of the beautiful and the sensual that carves him out of it and makes him vulnerable.

Many commentators have seen this poem as a source of inspiration for Edouard Manet's (1832–1883) revolutionary picture *Olympia* (FIG. 29). Like Baudelaire's temptress, Olympia is nude except for her jewels, has ''l'air vainqueur'' (''a conquering air''), the ''buste d'un imberbe'' (''the torso of a youth''), and has ''les yeux fixés sur moi, comme un tigre dompté'' (''her eyes fixed on me like those of a tamed tiger'').[30] Perhaps more than any other lines in the poem, ''la candeur unie à la lubricité / Donnait un charme neuf à ses métamorphoses'' (''her candor combined with her lubricity gave her metamorphoses a new charm'') characterize the painting. *Olympia*, like Baudelaire's poem, sparked outrage when it was presented, and for the same reason: the frankness of the sexuality. The great difference between Manet's odalisque and all those that preceded it, including Manet's starting point, Titian's *Venus d'Urbino*, who also wore only a bracelet as her adornment, was its defiant announcement of exactly who she was and what she was doing. Neither she nor the painter who created her was being dishonest. She is not a languorous, coy mistress but a nineteenth-century woman who knows what her business is. She is threatening because she has undergone a metamorphosis into something new and direct.

Manet had accepted Baudelaire's challenge to artists to recognize the marvelous in contemporary life. In so doing he fulfilled one of the requirements for becoming the true painter of modern life. Baudelaire asserted that, ''since all centuries and all peoples have had their own form of beauty, so inevitably we have ours. That is in the order of things.''[31] More specifically, he said, and undoubtedly his friend Manet was listening, ''the pageant of fashionable life and the thousands of floating existences — criminals and kept women — which drift about in the underworld of a great city . . . all prove to us that we have only to open our eyes to recognize our heroism.''[32] ''Le Peintre de la vie moderne'' was published while Manet was working on the painting and at a time when the painter and the poet were, if not constant companions, very close friends. In his essay Baudelaire wrote, ''If a painstaking, scrupulous,

30 Edouard Manet
Young Woman Reclining in a Spanish Costume, undated

but feebly imaginative artist has to paint a courtesan of today and takes his 'inspiration' (that is the accepted word) for a courtesan by Titian or Raphael, it is only too likely that he will produce a work which is false, ambiguous and obscure. From the study of a masterpiece of that time and type he will learn nothing of the bearing, the glance, the smile or the living 'style' of one of those creatures whom the dictionary of fashion has successively classified under the coarse or playful titles of 'doxies,' 'kept women,' *lorettes,* or *biches.*"[33] Some have speculated that Manet was trying to prove Baudelaire wrong by starting with a Renaissance model and showing he could make it modern.[34] More likely, he was being compliant rather than defiant, persisting in his habit of using a classical model but changing it radically so as to follow Baudelaire's prescription. The result is wonderfully successful in its combination of past and present to produce something new.

The spirit of Baudelaire is present in Manet's seminal work in several ways. Not only did his criticism stamp it with modernity, but his poetry infused it with ennui. Olympia has that look of knowing boredom on her face. She is aware that her state of detachment is derived from the constant and unfulfillable desire to satisfy desire, which in Baudelaire's view was characteristic not only of his age but of the human condition generally. For Baudelaire ennui is the infinite emotion: It "Prend les proportions de l'immortalité" (1:73; "takes on the proportions of immortality") and "ferait volontiers de la terres un débris / Et dans un bâillement avalerait le monde" (1:6; "would gladly turn the world into a wasteland and in a yawn swallow the world"). This theme, so consummately Baudelairean, becomes a distinguishing mark of Manet's women throughout his brilliant career. It appears in the downturned mouth and black eyes of his portrait of Jeanne Duval (FIG. 27), in the *Young Woman Reclining in a*

Spanish Costume (FIG. 30), painted just before *Olympia,* and in *At the Café* of 1878 (FIG. 53). In his grand masterpiece, *The Bar at the Folies-Bergère* (1881), painted two years before he died, the bar mistress's face exudes an ennui that casts a pall over the well-lit scene, as if the poet's spirit were hovering overhead.

Another woman also captivated both poet and painter. In 1862 a troupe of Spanish dancers performed at the Hippodrome in Paris, and every evening Baudelaire and Manet attended together to see the spectacular star Lola de Valence. Manet wanted to paint the dancers and arranged with the director of the company to have them pose for him. Of the several canvases that resulted, Baudelaire was most taken by the "marvelous" one of Lola herself (FIG. 31). He went so far as to write a quatrain that he wanted inscribed on the canvas, though it ended up on the frame of the painting and on the bottom of the etching Manet made after it.[35] Though Manet's friend Emile Zola did not believe, as many others did, that Manet's paintings were strongly influenced by Baudelaire's poetry, he did concede that this quatrain had "the great merit of summing up in rhyme the whole of the artist's individuality. It is perfectly true," he continued, "that *Lola de Valence* is a *bijou rose et noir.*"[36] The poet Paul Valéry did not agree. To him those "delicious" lines were "less appropriate to the strong and stocky *danseuse* . . . than to the cold and naked Olympia, that monster of banal sensuality."[37] Both were right. Zola's comment applies to the painting, with its jewel-like shimmer of colors so indicative of Manet's work. Valéry speaks of the woman. The poem reflects the duality Baudelaire always responded to in women as well as in beauty. Valéry rightly saw this quality more in Olympia than in Lola.

31 Edouard Manet
Lola de Valence, 1862

LOLA DE VALENCE

Entre tant de beautés que partout on peut voir,
Je comprends bien, amis, que le désir balance;
Mais on voit scintiller en Lola de Valence
Le charme inattendu d'un bijou rose et noir.

Among all the beauties one can see everywhere,
I understand, friends, that desire wavers;
but one sees glittering in Lola de Valence
the unexpected charm of a jewel, rose and black.

Primal Terror: Baudelaire and Edvard Munch

The affinity of Edvard Munch (1863–1944) for Baudelaire's poetry reveals much about both poet and painter. Between 1885 and 1896, Munch, a Norwegian, spent a considerable amount of time in France and toward the end of that period became involved with the school of Symbolist painters and poets. In 1896 he spent time with a number of intellectual and artistic figures associated with the Symbolist review *Mercure de France* and met and became friends with the Symbolist poet Stéphane Mallarmé. Baudelaire's poetry was seen in these circles as a major influence and was often read out loud at their gatherings, such as the famous Tuesday evenings at Mallarmé's apartment.

In April 1896 Munch received a commission from La Société des Cents Bibliophiles to make a set of illustrations for *Les Fleurs du mal*. It is a shame that the project was canceled shortly after its inception because of the death of the publisher, Alfred Piat. The result of an entirely conscious joining of word and visual image between two artists so much in sympathy would have been intriguing. Nevertheless, Munch did make three preparatory drawings, two of which bear titles of specific poems, "Le Mort joyeux" ("Joyful Death") and "Une Charogne" ("A Carrion") (FIG. 32), and a third called "Le Baiser — *Fleurs du mal*" ("The Kiss — *Flowers of Evil*"). Munch did not choose those two poems by chance. Both are concerned with what occurs after death, a subject Munch treated extensively in his writings and incorporated in his painting and printmaking, especially during this time. Just after he arrived in Paris for his first extended stay in November 1889, his father died. He was unable to return to Norway for the funeral but was deeply affected by the event, which had a long and profound effect on his work. From that point forward, the unity of life and death is a major theme in his art, and, to a significant extent, the manner in which he develops it derives from Baudelaire's poem "Une Charogne."

"Une Charogne" appealed to Munch because it also contains the idea of the unity of life and death in nature, as well as the notion that only the artist can preserve beauty, even if, as Baudelaire suggests in other places, he must die in the process. It is a powerful and shocking poem. As the poet and his beautiful mistress are strolling along a path, he points out a corpse rotting in the sun. The poet renders the corpse at once repulsive — "Les mouches bourdonnaient sur ce ventre putride, / D'où sortaient de noirs bataillons / De larves, qui coulaient comme un épais liquide / Le long de ces vivants haillons" ("The flies hummed on this putrid belly, from which came black battalions of worms, flowing like a thick liquid, bringing life to the tatters of clothing") — and beautiful — "Et ce monde rendait une étrange musique, / Comme l'eau courante et le vent, / Ou le grain qu'un vanneur d'un mouvement rythmique / Agite et tourne dans son van" ("And this world rendered a strange music, like the water flowing and the wind, or the grain that a winnower with rhythmic movement stirs and turns in his basket"). In fact, the repulsive and the beautiful are unified in the poem. It is difficult to know, however, exactly what Baudelaire's intention is. Does he wish to signify a unity in life in which the horrible and the beautiful are indissolubly bound to one another? Or does he inject a bitter irony, suggesting that even beauty's fate is only corruption? Toward the end of the poem, Baudelaire seems to fall into a reverie as he says that these images fade as if into a dream, as if they were a painter's sketch on a forgotten canvas that had emerged from the artist's memory. Finally he shakes himself free of fantasy and confronts his mistress with harsh reality. Someday you will be like this ordure, "Etoile de mes yeux, soleil de ma nature" ("star of my eyes, sun of my nature"):

Alors, ô ma beauté! dites à la vermine
   Qui vous mangera de baisers,
Que j'ai gardé la forme et l'essence divine
De mes amours décomposés!

Well, O my beauty! Tell the vermin who will eat you with their kisses that I have preserved the form and the divine essence of my decayed loves.

In these last lines Baudelaire is determined to inform his mistress as well as his reader that art is the only counter to our odious but inevitable fate, that resurrection of the spirit through poetry is the bulwark against the forces of decay.[38] This theme is revealed in Munch's work, in its incipient stage, in the preparatory drawings he did for *Les Fleurs du mal,* but its full-blown expression comes in the painting *Metabolism* and related drawings and prints (FIG. 33). *Metabolism* took him four years to complete (1895–1898), and he regarded it as so

32 Edvard Munch
A Carrion, c. 1896

Right page:
33 Edvard Munch
Metabolism, 1898

important that he described it as "the buckle for the belt" of the seminal series of works he called *The Frieze of Life*.[39]

The painting depicts two standing nudes, a young man and young woman facing each other, separated only by a tree trunk in the midst of a dark forest. Munch, however, reworked the painting many times, and X rays have revealed that, at one point, the figure of an embryo was emblazoned on the trunk of the tree. Moreover, its original frame, discovered after Munch's death, has a skeleton carved on the portion below the painting so that it appears to be buried beneath the standing couple and the tree.[40] This assemblage changes the reading of the painting from a simple representation of the vitality of youth surrounded by an ominous darkness to a picture of the cycle of life, death, decay, and regeneration that played

such a pivotal role in Munch's creative imagination during this period.

The work had multiple sources: the feelings and ideas stirred by the deaths of his father in 1889 and of his younger brother, Andreas, in 1895, a mural by Albert Besnard entitled *Life Reborn from Death* (1896), and, clearly, the poems on this subject by Baudelaire, especially "Une Charogne." The watercolor *Metabolism* portrays more clearly the theme of regeneration: the roots of the tree rise up out of the skeleton. Implicit here is the notion that regeneration takes place not only in nature but by means of art. Munch confirms this idea in his lithograph *The Urn* (FIG. 34), which goes beyond his preliminary drawing for "Une Charogne" as a full-fledged response to the poem. It evokes the concluding stanza of Baudelaire's poem by depicting the larger-than-life spirit of a woman rising out of an urn at whose base lie the bodies of women dead and dying, some even undergoing the process of decay. The urn symbolizes the power of the artist (whether poet or painter) to preserve the "divine essence" of his decaying loves through his art.

This correspondence between Munch and Baudelaire is reinforced even further when one notes the striking similarity between Munch's *Metabolism* and the illustration Baudelaire wanted used as the basis for the frontispiece of the 1861 edition of *Les Fleurs du mal*. It was a plate engraved by Eustache Hyacinthe Langlois that depicted Adam and Eve standing on either side of an arborescent skeleton (FIG. 35). In the original plate Langlois also included subterranean crypts containing bodies, making it even more similar to Munch's picture. No frontispiece drawing satisfactory to Baudelaire, who wanted an opening illustration that would emphasize the organic presence of sin within humankind, was created in time for the appearance of the second edition. However, a design based on the Langlois plate by the poet's

34 Edvard Munch, *The Urn,* 1896

friend Félicien Rops was used as a frontispiece for a later volume entitled *Les Epaves (The Waifs),* which appeared in 1866 and which contained, among other uncollected items, the poems banned from the first edition of *Les Fleurs du mal* (FIG. 36). It is not unlikely that Munch, given his involvement with Baudelaire's poetry during the time he was working on *Metabolism,* would have seen this book and Rops's etching.[41]

Munch and Baudelaire seem equally willing to portray starkly the horror of death, but finally there is an irony present in Baudelaire's work, at least in this poem, that is absent in Munch's. The painter's belief in a pantheistic regeneration seems to be his religion, his means of coping with the horror. He wrote that after death he would become one with the earth, "perpetually bathed in sunlight. . . . I would become one with it, and plants and trees would grow out of my rotting corpse. . . . I would be 'in' them, I would live on — that is eternity,"[42] and that is what he depicted in *Metabolism.* Salvation derives from a force outside of himself — the cycles of nature — and therefore awareness of it brings comfort in the face of death and decay. Baudelaire's poem provides no such external relief. The only salvation comes from his poetry because, as he put it, "It is one of the prodigious privileges of art that the horrible, artistically expressed, becomes beauty."[43] The circumstances of life itself, for Baudelaire, remain irreparable.

An equally powerful correspondence exists between the painter's most famous image, *The Scream* (FIG. 37), and a poem from *Les Fleurs du mal,* "Confession." In both Munch's picture and "Confession" a sudden and unexpected vocal expression is the climactic event: a plaintive and bizarre note wavering as it emerges in the poem, evidently a scream in the picture. In the poem, the time is just before dawn in Paris, and, just as in "Une Charogne," a man and a woman are walking together. In the picture, the time is dusk in Christiania (Oslo), Norway, and three people are standing on a bridge. The central figure is androgynous, looking a little like an aged child. In the poem the cry is made by the woman in the man's immediate presence. In the picture, although the two "friends" are nearby, the central figure is alone when the scream occurs. It is not clear if the central figure is literally screaming or reacting in horror to a scream going through nature.

The events in both works take place under a striking sky. Baudelaire's sky is tranquil, making the woman's wail even more shocking: "Il était tard; ainsi qu'une médaille neuve / La pleine lune s'étalait, / Et la solennité de la nuit, comme un fleuve, / Sur Paris dormant ruisselait" ("It was late; like a newly struck medallion, the full moon gleamed, and the solemnity of the night, like a river, flowed over sleeping Paris"). Munch's sky is pure terror, and if not the cause of the scream, then a reflection of it.

Despite these differences, the correspondence between the two works of art on the symbolic as well as the literal level is irresistible. In both an unexpected cry suddenly fills the atmosphere. The lines in Munch's sky are "tout en chancelant" ("powerfully wavering"), like the note that escapes from the poet's companion. Both sounds carry with them a sense of revelation, a revelation that comes from the deepest of sources. In both cases the shock that occurs as a result of the sound is as powerful as the sound itself, for as Baudelaire explains, the cry comes as if from "une enfant chétive, horrible, sombre, immonde, / Dont sa famille rougirait, / Et qu'elle aurait longtemps, pour la cacher au monde, / Dans un caveau mise au secret" ("a sickly child, horrible, somber, vile, who made her family blush and who, to keep her from the world, had long been hidden in a secret cave"). The shock the poet experiences at hearing his companion's

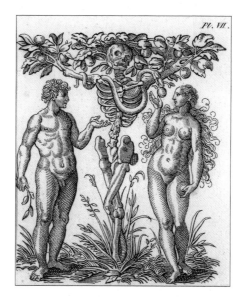

35 Eustache Hyacinthe Langlois
Adam and Eve, 1852

36 Félicien Rops
Frontispiece:
The Waifs, 1868

37 Edvard Munch
The Scream, 1895

"confidence horrible" is the confirmation of the universality of pain — even a beautiful woman cannot escape its clutches. "Que c'est un dur métier que d'être belle femme" ("that it is a hard lot being a beautiful woman"). The poet, who had always longed for such beauty and for a woman who possessed it, is haunted by her cry and "cette lune enchantée, / Ce silence et cette langueur, / Et cette confidence horrible chuchotée / Au confessionnal du cœur" ("that enchanted moon, that silence and that languor, and that horrible confidence whispered in the confessional of the heart"). For Munch, it is as though the shock of his revelation has caused him to undergo a metamorphosis and emerge as the terrified and terrifying child in Baudelaire's poem. Munch's revelation is less specific, but the scream seems to carry with it that which is most horrifying about human existence. As Baudelaire wrote to his mother that he had always been damned and would always be, so Munch wrote, "the terror of life has pursued me ever since I first began to

Tout à coup, au milieu de l'intimité libre
    Éclose à la pâle clarté,
De vous, riche et sonore instrument où ne vibre
    Que la radieuse gaieté,

De vous, claire et joyeuse ainsi qu'une fanfare
    Dans le matin étincelant,
Une note plaintive, une note bizarre
    S'échappa tout en chancelant

Comme une enfant chétive, horrible, sombre, immonde,
    Dont sa famille rougirait,
Et qu'elle aurait longtemps, pour la cacher au monde,
    Dans un caveau mise au secret.

Pauvre ange, elle chantait, votre note criarde:
    "Que rien ici-bas n'est certain,
Et que toujours, avec quelque soin qu'il se farde,
    Se trahit l'égoïsme humain."

From "Confession"

Suddenly, in the midst of our intimacy,
    blooming in the pale light,
from your normally rich and sonorous voice,
    where only radiant delight

clear and joyous
    as the sparkling morn
had quivered, a sorrowful and bizarre note
    escaped, mightily wavering

as if from a sickly child, horrible, somber, vile,
    who made her family blush
and who, to keep her from the world,
    had long been hidden in a secret cave.

Poor angel, from your piercing note came:
    "Nothing here below is certain,
and though a mask is put on daily,
    human egotism cannot be hidden."

From "Confession"

think."[44] In "Confession" and *The Scream,* poet and painter reaffirm their common belief in the depth of human vulnerability to that terror.[45]

One of the themes that permeates *Les Fleurs du mal* and the series of prints Munch called *The Frieze of Life* is the anguish of the tortured relationships with women experienced by both poet and painter. Like Baudelaire, Munch had a divided view of women. In 1894 he described woman as being "at the same time a saint, a whore and a hapless devotée,"[46] a phrase that recalls Baudelaire's notion of woman as "divine and infernal."

In "Le Vampire," the poet, metaphorically identifies a woman — "Toi" ("you") — with the vampire of the title. He also equates the "Toi" figure with the stroke of a dagger entering his plaintive heart and with a troupe of demons. He pleads with himself to commit suicide as the only means of release from the suffering that this figure is inflicting on him.[47] At the end of the poem, a reversal reveals the truth. Death informs him that he himself is the guilty party. The vampire is really a symbol of his own lust, his addiction to sin. If the vampire were destroyed, he would only resuscitate it with his own kisses. The misogyny is mitigated to some degree by this final revelation, but

Toi qui, comme un coup de couteau,
Dans mon cœur plaintif es entrée;
Toi qui, forte comme un troupeau
De démons, vins, folle et parée,

De mon esprit humilié
Faire ton lit et ton domaine;
— Infame à qui je suis lié
Comme le forçat à la chaîne,

Comme au jeu le joueur têtu,
Comme à la bouteille l'ivrogne,
Comme aux vermines la charogne,
— Maudite, maudite sois-tu!

From "Le Vampire"

You who entered my plaintive heart
like the thrust of the knife;
you who, powerful as a herd
of demons, wild and ready,

made your bed and your domain
in my humiliated self
— Infamous one to whom I am tied
like a convict to a chain,

like a gambler to his game,
like the drunkard to his bottle,
like vermin to a corpse,
— cursed one, be damned.

From "The Vampire"

38 Edvard Munch
Vampire, 1895

it cannot be ignored that in the process of reaching it the woman is vilified. It is, after all, she, in the form of a vampire, who, as the poem recounts, has made her bed in his spirit and bound herself to him "comme aux vermines la charogne" ("like vermin to a corpse").

Munch's *Vampire* (FIG. 38) was the third picture in the original *Frieze of Life*. Munch claimed that the picture was "just a woman kissing a man on the neck,"[48] but the remark seems disingenuous when one sees the way the woman's blood-like red hair drips down over the man and envelops him, and considers that the picture was first called *Love and Pain,* which certainly would have been an appropriate title for Baudelaire's poem as well. It is also belied by the other harpy/vampire images in Munch's œuvre (FIG. 39). A passage Munch wrote describing the picture seems to confirm his Baudelairean ambivalence toward women: "And he lay his head against her breast — he felt the blood rush in her veins — he listened to her heartbeat — He buried his face in her lap — he felt two burning lips in the back of his neck — it gave him a freezing sensation through his body — a freezing lust — Then he pressed her forcefully toward him."[49] As Rodolphe Rapetti, in his catalogue essay for the exhibition *Munch et La France,* states, "The theme of the *Vampire* which Munch takes up in painting as well as in printmaking appears in *Les Fleurs du mal* with a significance exactly identical to that realized by the artist."[50]

Je suis belle: *Baudelaire and Auguste Rodin*

The outward persona of Auguste Rodin (1840–1917) — robust, confident, dominant if not domineering — contrasts sharply with that of Baudelaire — frail, irascible, often defensive if not defiant. Nevertheless, a deep vein of sympathy runs between the underlying essence of Rodin's art and Baudelaire's poetry. This is true not only

39 Edvard Munch
Harpy, 1900

Et, quand je m'ennuierai de ces farces impies,
Je poserai sur lui ma frêle et forte main;
Et mes ongles, pareils aux ongles des harpies,
Sauront jusqu'à son cœur se frayer un chemin.

From "Bénédiction"

And when I am bored with these impious appeals,
I will lay my frail but powerful hand upon him,
and my nails, like those of harpies,
will know how to dig out a path to his very heart.

From "Benediction"

in regard to their view of women as a source of both inspiration and destructive torment but of themselves as artists mirroring the fate of all men: alone, spiritually empty, and bent on a self-destructive quest for ideals they cannot reach. Rodin acknowledged this sympathy many times.

He inscribed the first quatrain of Baudelaire's poem "La Beauté" on the base of his sculpture *Je suis belle (I Am Beautiful)* (FIG. 40). The title of Rodin's work is itself the first three words of Baudelaire's poem.[51] Although Georges Rouault's etching and aquatint illustrating "La Beauté" (FIG. 41) forcefully communicates the hardness in beauty, Rodin's sculpture is actually made of the stone against which Baudelaire's poets, one after the other, meet their demise. The sculptor's dream, fashioned in stone, symbolizes the eternal frustration of the lover pursuing the unsubmissive woman and of the artist pursuing the unattainable ideal. The poem and the sculpture are confessions of vain strivings for perfection in art. This is made all the more poignant for Rodin because he was unable to finish his monumental work *The Gates of Hell,* which, like *Les Fleurs du mal,* is an allegory of the human condition.[52] According to Albert Elsen, "A study of *The Gates* is aided by a rereading of the poetry of Baudelaire, upon which Rodin drew for inspiration and for the articulation of feelings that he shared with the poet."[53] What joins the work of the two men is that both "dealt with mankind, adrift in the empire of the night; . . . [were] born with a fatal duality of desire and an incapacity to fulfill it; [and were] damned on both sides of the tomb to an internal hell of passions. The dialectic of movement and inertia set the same beat for the personages in Baudelaire's poems and in Rodin's sculpture."[54] Judith Cladel is more graphic in the description of the correspondence between the two works: "Dante inspired this monstrous yet ennobled masterpiece, and Baudelaire's poetry filled many of its

40 Auguste Rodin
I Am Beautiful, 1882

LA BEAUTÉ

Je suis belle, ô mortels! comme un rêve de pierre,
Et mon sein, où chacun s'est meurtri tour à tour,
Est fait pour inspirer au poëte un amour
Éternel et muet ainsi que la matière.

Je trône dans l'azur comme un sphinx incompris;
J'unis un cœur de neige à la blancheur des cygnes;
Je hais le mouvement qui déplace les lignes,
Et jamais je ne pleure et jamais je ne ris.

Les poëtes, devant mes grandes attitudes,
Que j'ai l'air d'emprunter aux plus fiers monuments,
Consumeront leurs jours en d'austères études;

Car j'ai, pour fasciner ces dociles amants,
De purs miroirs qui font toutes choses plus belles:
Mes yeux, mes larges yeux aux clartés éternelles!

BEAUTY

I am beautiful, O mortals, like a dream in stone,
and my breast, where each dies in his turn,
is made to inspire in the poet a love
eternal and silent as the stone itself.

I am enthroned in the azure like an incomprehensible
sphinx; in me a heart of snow blends with the whiteness
of a swan; I hate the movement that displaces the lines,
and I never cry and I never laugh.

The poets, before my lofty pose,
which I borrow from the proudest monuments,
consume their days in austere study,

for I fascinate these docile lovers with
mirrors making everything more beautiful: my eyes,
my huge eyes, are filled with eternal bursts of light.

41 Georges Rouault
Beauty, 1926–1927

Right page:
42 Auguste Rodin
De Profundis Clamavi,
1887–1888

chinks and crannies with ignoble writhing shapes; shapes of dusky fire that, as they tumultuously stand above the gulf of fear, wave ineffectual and desperate hands as if imploring destiny."[55]

Rodin's most direct response to Baudelaire came in 1887, when the publisher Paul Gallimard asked him to illustrate his copy of the first edition of *Les Fleurs du mal.* Rodin made twenty-two drawings directly on the pages of Gallimard's copy and five others on separate sheets[56] that were inserted into the volume. Some of Rodin's drawings are the visual record of his responses to the poems at the time he illustrated them, while others are based on the earlier inspiration Rodin received from Baudelaire while working on *The Gates of Hell* or on other sculptures inspired by the poet. For example, the drawing for the poem "De profundis clamavi" ("Out of the Depths I Have Cried") (FIG. 42) derives from *Je suis belle,* on which Rodin inscribed the lines from "La Beauté." That Rodin used a drawing associated with his frustrations in creating art to illustrate a poem about the nadir of human despair makes his sympathy with the central paradox of Baudelaire's poetry all the more clear. At the bottom of this drawing he quoted these lines from "De profundis clamavi": "J'implore ta pitié, Toi, l'unique que j'aime, / Du fond du gouffre obscure où mon cœur est tombé" ("I implore your pity, You, the only one whom I love, from the depths of the dark abyss where my heart has fallen").[57] As in so many of Baudelaire's poems, desire, whether for a woman or for ideal beauty, is the cause for the plunge into the abyss. Yet, ironically, it is to the very object of desire that the speaker applies for salvation.

The Fall of Icarus:
Bruegel, Goltzius, Matisse

Another poem that focuses on this painfully ironic quest for beauty is "Les Plaintes d'un Icare" ("The Laments of an Icarus"). Here Baudelaire turns to Greek mythology for the irony that resides at the center of so much of his life and art: the more the poet pursues the ideal, the more certain is his doom. In the poem, those who seek out the vulgar, "lovers of prostitutes," for instance, seem blessed; those who try to soar above the commonplace are blinded by the brightness and broken by the elusiveness of what they seek. And since it records the laments of an Icarus, the poem implies that all artists who seek the heights of beauty are fated to fall.

A number of sources underlie "The Laments of an Icarus." The most obvious is the Icarus story in Ovid's *Metamorphoses,* which Baudelaire would have read in school since he was a particularly accomplished Latin scholar. Ovid tells of Daedalus, who was tired of his exile in Crete and wanted to go home to Greece. Knowing that King Minos controlled all escape routes except the air, he used his expert craftsmanship to build wings for his son, Icarus, and himself. After warning his son to fly a middle course, neither too close to the sky nor too close to the sea, the two departed.

LES PLAINTES D'UN ICARE

Les amants des prostituées
Sont heureux, dispos et repus;
Quant à moi, mes bras sont rompus
Pour avoir étreint des nuées.

C'est grâce aux astres nonpareils,
Qui tout au fond du ciel flamboient,
Que mes yeux consumés ne voient
Que des souvenirs de soleils.

En vain j'ai voulu de l'espace
Trouver la fin et le milieu;
Sous je ne sais quel œil de feu
Je sens mon aile qui se casse;

Et brûlé par l'amour du beau,
Je n'aurai pas l'honneur sublime
De donner mon nom à l'abîme
Qui me servira de tombeau.

THE LAMENTS OF AN ICARUS

Lovers of prostitutes
are happy, fresh, and satisfied;
as for me, my arms are broken
for having embraced the clouds.

It is thanks to the unequaled stars,
which blaze within the deepest sky,
that my burned-out eyes can see
only the suns of memory.

In vain I wished to seek out
the center and the boundary of space;
under some unknown fiery eye
I felt my wings break;

And burned by the love of beauty,
I will never have the sublime honor
of giving my name to the abyss
that will serve as my tomb.

43 Hendrik Goltzius
Icarus, 1588

But in his quest to reach the heights, Icarus soared too near the sun. The wax that held his fragile wings together melted, and he plunged into the sea. Much in Ovid's rendition must have had particular poignancy for Baudelaire. The emphasis on the relationship between father and son would certainly have affected him: "Even as his lips were crying his father's name, they were swallowed up in the deep blue waters which are called after him."[58] Given the impact of Baudelaire's early loss of his own father, it is no wonder that this story is the underpinning for a poem that metaphorically accounts for the disappointments and frustrations in his life. In the poem Baudelaire sees his own fate as even worse than that of Icarus, who may have plunged into the sea, but at least had that sea named after him. Baudelaire, perhaps ironically, says, "Je n'aurai pas l'honneur sublime / De donner mon nom à l'abîme / Qui me servira de tombeau." ("I will never have the sublime honor of giving my name to the abyss that will serve as my tomb"). Ultimately, he was wrong, of course,

for posterity has not denied him the fame he desired.

Other possible sources for Baudelaire's Icarus are in the visual versions of Ovid's story created by the Flemish painter and engraver Pieter Bruegel the Elder (c. 1525–1569). Through engravings, Baudelaire was familiar with the complete works of Bruegel, so he must have seen one or more of his Icarus pieces. The most famous one, the one that later inspired poets such as W. H. Auden and William Carlos Williams,[59] is *The Fall of Icarus* (FIG. 44). Here Icarus disappears beneath the waves as all sorts of commonplace activities occur in the vicinity: fishermen are fishing, farmers are plowing, a ship is sailing. No one even notices what has happened to the heroic but foolish boy. Just as in Baudelaire's poem, lovers of the commonplace are blessed, but Icarus is doomed.[60]

In another Bruegel picture Icarus is still airborne, still above his father, who has lost sight of him and is searching for him. They are both dwarfed by a passing ship. Again Bruegel places the emphasis on the mundane, while foiled heroism and tragedy play a diminutive role in the background. Baudelaire would have had little trouble envisioning his own unacknowledged heroism — the poet trying to tell the truth to an unconcerned and ignorant world — in such a scene.

Another sixteenth-century Flemish artist who took up the Icarus theme and whose work Baudelaire certainly knew was the engraver Hendrik Goltzius (1558–1617).[61] From his series of four "imprudents" — Tantalus, Icarus, Phaeton, and Ixion — Baudelaire apparently drew upon elements of both Icarus and Ixion for "Les Plaintes d'un Icare" (FIG. 43). Goltzius's Icarus is plummeting into the sea, his hand covering eyes burned out by the sun, just like Baudelaire's Icarus. And Goltzius's inscription for his Ixion engraving tells us that Ixion, who took to the heavens to seduce Juno, wound up hugging only the clouds, the same clouds that break the poet's arms.[62] As he does in "La Béatrice," "Les Phares," and a number of other poems, Baudelaire amalgamates images from various sources to meet the demands of his own imagination.

44 Pieter Bruegel the Elder
The Fall of Icarus, c. 1558

45 Henri Matisse, *Icarus,* 1943

More than three centuries after Bruegel and Goltzius, Henri Matisse's (1869–1954) preoccupation with the figure of Icarus is closely connected to Baudelaire as well. In 1943 and 1944 Matisse created at least five figures of the mythical boy who fell from the heights. The most well known is the work entitled *Icarus* (FIG. 45) that appeared on the cover and as plate VIII in Matisse's *Jazz.* A similar picture, *The Fall of Icarus,* was the frontispiece for the important 1945 issue of *Verve* (FIG. 46). Two others were created specifically to illustrate Baudelaire's "Les Plaintes d'un Icare" (FIGS. 47, 48).

During the war years, Matisse had undergone serious surgery, and members of his family had been imprisoned for their efforts in the Resistance. These years were difficult for him, and the prospect of a great fall must have seemed possible, if not likely. Interpreters of Matisse have suggested that the war swirling around him and his personal difficulties were the inspiration for the bursting stars that surround the *Jazz* Icarus. The flashes, they claim, are not just his version of the sun Icarus approached but also represent the shells that on at least one occasion burst in the sky near his residence in Vence on the Côte d'Azur to which he had fled from Paris and Nice.

At the time when Matisse was creating all these Icarus figures, he was also deeply involved in the process of illustrating Baudelaire. In September 1944, after many months of work, Matisse finally completed more than thirty drawings. They were all faces designed to accompany specific poems in a proposed limited edition of *Les Fleurs du mal.* But then an odd accident occurred. The drawings, designed to be transferred from special paper to lithographic plates, were slightly altered by humidity. For the perfectionist Matisse, they were rendered useless. Discouraged but no less determined to complete the project, he started over. He had completed the better part of a new series before he decided that they were not right either. Somehow they were different from the first set, different from his original response to Baudelaire. Fortunately, he had made photographs of the originals before they were damaged, and the decision was made to publish the book with lithographs made from them.[63]

The writer Louis Aragon dissuaded Matisse from discarding the second set of drawings and even convinced him to issue a small edition of lithographs made from them. One drawing in the second set was another face to accompany "Les Plaintes d'un Icare." It was, however, significantly different from the first version. Both are heads of a young man. In the original the face of Icarus is benign and androgynous (FIG. 47). In the second, Matisse has altered the curvature of his lines ever so slightly so that Icarus has become defiant and angry (FIG. 48). The difference is too strong to be accounted for by a chance stroke of the lithographic crayon, especially by a draftsman as exacting as Matisse. The explanation for the difference lies in two Matisse portraits of Baudelaire himself that reveal a parallel in the artist's mind between Icarus and Baudelaire on the one hand and between both of them and himself on the other. The first is the famous etching of a scowling Baudelaire done to accompany Mallarmé's poem "Le Tombeau de Baudelaire" ("Baudelaire's Tomb" or "Tribute to Baudelaire") (FIG. 49). No other portrait of Baudelaire captures so well the defiant and embittered character of the poet. The other comes from Matisse's first set of lithographs for *Les Fleurs du mal,* showing a youthful and innocent Baudelaire (FIG. 98). Apparently Matisse had two conceptions of Baudelaire in his artistic consciousness just as he had two conceptions of Icarus, one innocent and at ease, the other angry and tormented. The two perspectives can be taken as a reflection of a dualistic view of himself as well. The first parallels his long-held view that

46 Henri Matisse, *The Fall of Icarus,* 1945

47 Henri Matisse, *Laments of an Icarus,* 1944

48 Henri Matisse, *Laments of an Icarus,* 1946

he was an artist who wanted people who were weary and stressed "to find peace and tranquillity as they looked at [his] pictures." The second recalls the enormous strain Matisse was under at the time, in a sense trapped and facing a future of decline, as Daedalus and Icarus had been on Crete. His differing views of Icarus and Baudelaire correspond to the contrast between the peace he had known for most of his own life and the frustration of his present circumstances, between the "luxe, calme et volupté" of so much of his work and the crackling tension that informs so many of his self-portraits as well as other works rooted in autobiography. (See, for example, *The Woman with the Hat* [1905], *The Green Line* [1905], *Self-Portrait* [1906], and *The Conversation* [1908–1910].)[64]

Baudelaire says, "C'est grâce aux astres nonpareils, / Qui tout au fond du ciel flamboient, / Que mes yeux consumés ne voient / Que des souvenirs de soleils" ("It is thanks to the unequaled stars, which blaze within the deepest sky, that my burned-out eyes can see only the suns of memory"). For Baudelaire these memories are the lost paradise of childhood, a craving for the wholeness that was not available in his adult life. Matisse also turned to memory as a counter to the distress of the present and created Icarus without eyes (FIGS. 45, 46) forcing an inward focus. Moreover, one of these Icaruses (FIG. 46) not only is surrounded by brilliant flashes as he plunges into the abyss, but has a heart that *is* one of those flashes. It is an interior sun, exactly parallel to one of Baudelaire's suns of memory. Critic Pierre Schneider points to this correspondence when he writes, "His [Matisse's] remedy against the times, discovered by all accounts during the period of his operation and its aftermath of enforced immobility, was the power of recollection: 'I'm growing old, I delight in the past!'"[65] The multiple flares in the sky of Baudelaire's poem are carried over in

49 Henri Matisse, *Portrait of Baudelaire*, 1932

the multiple flashes in Matisse's sky. These dangerous skies were omnipresent in Baudelaire's life and work. Late in his life when Matisse found himself threatened by them, he quite naturally found himself in great sympathy with the poet.

L'Irréparable:
Daumier, Rouault, and Other Artists

When the poet falls from these dangerous skies having failed to reach his ideal, he finds himself back in the world confronting the unrelenting state of sin that engenders remorse and ennui, bereft of all that might provide relief from suffering. In short he faces "L'Irréparable." In his poem of that title, Baudelaire is again traveling into the depths, and illusions of flight disintegrate even more quickly than they do for Icarus. A number of artists have produced works that correspond to his images in "L'Irréparable." Rodin illustrated its opening image by transforming the "long Remords, / Qui vit, s'agite et se tortille, / Et se nourrit de nous comme le ver des morts" ("longstanding Remorse that lives, agitates, and writhes — that nourishes itself within us like the worm in the dead") into a single, coiling snake wrapped around the torso of a man. He has externalized the remorse in his visual metaphor (FIG. 50).

The image at the poem's center is that of voyagers. They are traveling under "un ciel bourbeux et noir . . . / Plus denses que la poix, sans matin et sans soir" ("a sky muddy and black . . . denser than pitch, without morning and without evening"). They search futilely for hope on a road leading inevitably to Hell. Honoré Daumier (1808–1879), Baudelaire's friend and kindred spirit, pondered exiles and wayfarers repeatedly in his paintings, drawings, and reliefs. In *The Fugitives* (FIG. 51), it is as if Daumier has assembled his outcasts — his beggars, his *saltimbanques,* his worn-out old women (the same victims of life that populate Baudelaire's "Tableaux parisiens" — and

L'IRRÉPARABLE

Pouvons-nous étouffer le vieux, le long Remords,
    Qui vit, s'agite et se tortille,
Et se nourrit de nous comme le ver des morts,
    Comme du chêne la chenille?
Pouvons-nous étouffer l'implacable Remords?

Dans quel philtre, dans quel vin, dans quelle tisane,
    Noierons-nous ce vieil ennemi,
Destructeur et gourmand comme la courtisane,
    Patient comme la fourmi?
Dans quel philtre? — dans quel vin? — dans quelle
    tisane?

THE IRREPARABLE

How can we suffocate this ancient, this long-standing
    Remorse that lives, agitates, and writhes
— that nourishes itself within us like the worm in the dead,
    like the caterpillar on the oak?
How can we suffocate this implacable Remorse?

In what drug, in what wine, in what tea
    can we drown this old enemy,
greedier and more destructive than a whore,
    more patient than an ant?
— In what drug, in what wine, in what tea?

Left page:
50 Auguste Rodin
L'Irréparable, 1887–1888

51 Honoré Daumier
The Fugitives, c. 1868

of the typical way stations on this road, the cheap theater where he remembers an illusion of relief, having seen there on a banal stage a magical creature in whom he puts his faith for a few deceptive moments. The scene of the Parisian theater in which a lonely man gazes at a woman on a stage, a dim hope brightly reflected in his eyes, on his face, or in his posture, has been repeated by painter after painter in the generations following Baudelaire. Manet (FIG. 53), Degas, Munch, Toulouse-Lautrec, and Seurat (FIG. 52), among others, all have their versions. At first glance they are only the vibrantly colored representations of the café concert or the Folies-Bèrgere, repositories of the vitality or the decadence, depending upon one's point of view, that is characteristic of an era. But after one reads Baudelaire's poem, these pictures become rich and deeply felt symbols of the tragedy of the human heart played out in the artificially lit urban theater, the one place on the voyager's path that appears to provide light but finally reveals only the darkness of his own soul.

Georges Rouault's (1871–1958) response to "L'Irréparable" emerges from a deeply felt empathy with Baudelaire. In his *Souvenirs intimes* the artist wrote that he recognized in Baudelaire "the affectionate smile of a brother of the spirit."[66] As further testament to this affinity, he made his tortured lithographic portrait of the poet (FIG. 8) the frontispiece for his diary when it was published. Rouault read Baudelaire throughout his life. His daughters report that there was always a copy of *Les Fleurs du mal* and *Le Spleen de Paris* on his bedside table and that he often spontaneously quoted lines to them "as if they touched some powerful chord in his innermost being."[67] Figures of lost women, sad clowns, weary working people, and exiles wander through Rouault's paintings just as they do in Baudelaire's poems. And like Baudelaire, he shocked people. The shadows stretching across his canvases and prints were just

53 Edouard Manet
At the Café, 1878

set them down on the "chemin mauvais" ("woeful road") that stretches toward eternity. The very angle at which Daumier inclines the refugees in relation to their tortuous path signifies that "L'Espérance qui brille aux carreaux de l'Auberge / Est soufflée, est morte à jamais!" ("The Hope that shines in the windows of the Inn is blown out, is dead forever!").

At the end of the poem Baudelaire visits one

too long for many, such as his great friend and supporter the Catholic visionary writer Léon Bloy, who ultimately felt that "the poor devil [had] taken a leap into utter darkness."[68] With greater insight, critic Pierre Courthion understood that "Because he [Rouault] saw things darkly, he painted darkly. Tortuous contours and ungainly forms were charged with revealing the raw physical nature of sin. . . . It was a journey into Hell, but with faith in redemption."[69]

That journey, with the exception of the redemption at its end, is strikingly similar to Baudelaire's. Rouault, who was more consistently and traditionally Christian than Baudelaire, understood that though the poet did not allow for salvation in much of his work, he was nevertheless deeply spiritual. The painter wrote, "Although men like Baudelaire and Verlaine may appear to some to have fallen very low, they nevertheless retain so much natural distinction (in comparison with those who censure them . . .) and give off so spiritual a fragrance that they need but a word or a glance to put everything in its proper perspective."[70] The poet and the artist stand together, practically alone among the moderns, in asserting the existence of Evil, while at the same time pouring out compassion for all, because all are in its embrace. Of the many prints and paintings Rouault created in direct response to *Les Fleurs du mal,* none evokes this suffering and compassion more powerfully than the face he etched to illustrate "L'Irréparable" (FIG. 54). On that face is the expression of the poet who laments despairingly, "mon cœur, que jamais ne visite l'extase, / Est un théâtre où l'on attend / Toujours, toujours en vain, l'Etre aux ailes de gaze!" ("ecstacy will never visit my heart; my heart is a theater where one waits forever for the appearance of the Being with wings of gauze!")

54 Georges Rouault, *The Irreparable (Satan III),* 1926–1927

55 Edvard Munch
Rue Lafayette, 1891

Voyage into the City

Baudelaire and Paris were on intimate terms. His relationship with the city, though ambivalent, was the closest and most successful of his life. In 1853 the editor Fernand Desnoyers wrote to Baudelaire asking him for some "poems on nature." Apparently irritated by Desnoyer's ignorance of his distaste for barbarous and depraved nature and his strong preference for things urban, he responded, "I'll never believe that the soul of the gods inhabits plants, and even if it did, I really couldn't work up much enthusiasm for the fact and would consider my own soul as of much more importance than that of the sanctified vegetables."[1] Instead, he sent two of his great city poems, "Le Crépuscule du soir" ("Evening Twilight") and "Le Crépuscule du matin" ("Morning Twilight"). He concluded his letter by picturing nature as a place to worship the city: "In the depths of the woods, shut in by those vaults that recall sacristies and cathedrals, I think of our amazing cities." His urban creed is reinforced by his call to artists to paint the city because "The life of our city is rich in poetic and marvelous subjects. We are enveloped and steeped as though in an atmosphere of the marvelous; but we do not notice it."[2] Similarly, he implored landscapists to turn their attention to the "great cities, by which I mean that collection of grandeurs and beauties which results from a powerful agglomeration of men and monuments — that profound and complex charm of a capital city which has grown old and aged in the glories and the tribulations of life."[3]

His view of the city was not always so sanguine. At a given moment those tribulations for which the city was both setting and symbol in his poems could cause him to want nothing more than to leave it. In "Moesta et errabunda," one of his beautiful escapist poems, he ponders being whisked away from "l'immonde cité" ("the squalid city"), a place where "la boue est faite de nos pleurs" ("the mud is made with our tears"). In 1859 he wrote to Victor Hugo, in exile on the island of Guernsey, "I'm also informed that you feel regret and nostalgia. That information may be wrong. But if it is true, a single day in our sad, boring Paris, our Paris–New York, would achieve a radical cure. If I didn't have some tasks to perform here I'd go to the ends of the world."[4] This ambivalence about the city reflects his attitude toward himself and life and is the wellspring for the tense energy in his poetry. For Baudelaire, the city was the most compelling entity outside the nature of the human soul itself. Indeed, he referred to "l'ivresse religieuse des grandes villes" (1:651; "the religious intoxication of great cities"). The city is often his metaphor for the paradoxical complexities of the human being and the human condition as well as his single greatest source of inspiration. It is a paradigm for all that is beautiful and all that is ugly, a place where ugliness reveals its own beauty, where "toute énormité fleurit comme une fleur" (1:191; "every outrage blossoms like a flower"). For the modern painters and poets who took their cues from Baudelaire the city supplied the aesthetic and substantive underpinnings for art in the way that nature had for the Romantics in the generation before his.

At the same time Baudelaire was urging painters, in his critical essays, to take up the city as their subject, he was immersing them in its beautiful and terrible essence in his poetry. His vision helped shape the way generations of painters and poets regarded the city. Even Impressionism, a style not readily associated with Baudelaire's gritty urban evocations, was in a fashion an urban form because it partook of the landscape qualities of

56 Claude Monet
Arrival of the Normandy Train, Saint Lazare Station, 1877

the city that Baudelaire had pointed out. As Arnold Hauser noted, Impressionism "is an urban style because it describes the changeability, the nervous rhythm, the sudden sharp but always ephemeral impressions of the city."[5] In this sense Impressionism, in the city paintings of Manet, Monet, and Pissarro, is Baudelairean because it catches the "fugitive fleeting beauty of our present-day life, that quality which . . . we have called 'modernity'" (FIG. 56).[6] Most of the artists in tune with Baudelaire's vision of the city were not Impressionists, however. They were artists who probed deeper than the shimmering surface to discover the sad, dark heart of the modern city.

The City as Landscape: Baudelaire and Charles Méryon

An artist whose poetic rendering of the city Baudelaire admired greatly was the etcher Charles Méryon (1821–1868). Similarities between Baudelaire and Méryon are numerous. Both were Parisians, born in the same year. Both sailed to southern seas as young men. Méryon became a seaman to earn a living; Baudelaire set sail because his authoritarian stepfather, Jacques Aupick, wanted to curb his profligacy by removing him from the nefarious influences of Paris and to steer him away from writing poetry. Aupick, an up-and-coming military man later to become a general, a senator, and an ambassador, wrote to Baudelaire's older half-brother, a bourgeois lawyer, with an irony neither could have appreciated. If he couldn't keep the boy from becoming a poet, he said, he could at least make him into "a poet who could draw his inspiration from better springs than the sewers of Paris."[7] Neither Méryon nor

PAYSAGE

Je veux, pour composer chastement mes églogues,
Coucher auprès du ciel, comme les astrologues,
Et, voisin des clochers, écouter en rêvant
Leurs hymnes solennels emportés par le vent.
Les deux mains au menton, du haut de ma mansarde,
Je verrai l'atelier qui chante et qui bavarde;
Les tuyaux, les clochers, ces mâts de la cité,
Et les grands ciels qui font rêver d'éternité.

Il est doux, à travers les brumes, de voir naître
L'étoile dans l'azur, la lampe à la fenêtre,
Les fleuves de charbon monter au firmament
Et la lune verser son pâle enchantement.
Je verrai les printemps, les étés, les automnes,
Et quand viendra l'hiver aux neiges monotones,
Je fermerai partout portières et volets
Pour bâtir dans la nuit mes féeriques palais.
Alors je rêverai des horizons bleuâtres,
Des jardins, des jets d'eau pleurant dans les albâtres,
Des baisers, des oiseaux chantant soir et matin,
Et tout ce que l'Idylle a de plus enfantin.
L'Émeute, tempêtant vainement à ma vitre,
Ne fera pas lever mon front de mon pupitre;
Car je serai plongé dans cette volupté
D'évoquer le Printemps avec ma volonté,
De tirer un soleil de mon cœur, et de faire
De mes pensers brûlants une tiède atmosphère.

LANDSCAPE

I wish, in order to compose my eclogues purely,
to sleep close to heaven as do the astrologers,
neighbor to the bell towers, and to hear, while dreaming,
their solemn hymns carried by the wind.
From high in my attic, my two hands under my chin,
I will see down below chattering workshops,
chimneys, steeples, these masts of the city,
and those sweeping skies that provoke dreams of eternity.

It is sweet to see through the mists the star
being born in the azure, the lamp in the window,
the rivers of smoke climbing to the heavens,
and the moon pouring its pale enchantment.
I will see springtimes, summers, and autumns;
and when winter's snowy monotones arrive,
I will close my windows, latch my shutters,
and build magical realms in the night.
Then I will dream of cerulean horizons
and of gardens, of fountains crying into alabaster,
of kisses and birds singing from dawn to dusk
— of the most childlike idylls.
Riot raging at my window
will not turn my head from my desk;
for I shall immerse myself in this ecstasy,
and with my will, draw forth the spring,
create a sun from my heart,
and from my ardent fancy a balmy clime.

57 Charles Méryon
Le Stryge, 1853

Baudelaire was successful by bourgeois standards. Both were eccentric men with lives characterized by recurring poverty and isolation, and they died destitute within a year of each other. Méryon's death occurred after years in and out of mental institutions. Baudelaire, speechless for months after a stroke, died from advanced syphilis. The city that nourished their art tortured them in their day-to-day existence, an irony that the poet certainly felt but also appreciated.

Méryon has often been called the greatest of French etchers. His most famous set of etchings, entitled *Eaux-fortes sur Paris (Etchings on Paris),* was published in 1857, the same year as the first edition of *Les Fleurs du mal.* In many ways his pictures could have been companion pieces for Baudelaire's city poems, the "Tableaux parisiens," which first appeared together as a chapter in the sec-

ond edition of *Les Fleurs du mal* in 1861.[8] In fact, Méryon's etchings may have in an odd way motivated Baudelaire to create that chapter. Baudelaire was so taken by Méryon's renderings of "des points de vue poétiques de Paris" ("the poetical points of view of Paris")[9] (FIGS. 57, 58, 62) that he offered to write some poems to accompany a future edition. He loved the thought of "some reveries of ten or twenty or thirty lines inspired by beautiful engravings, the philosophical reveries of a stroller in Paris."[10] Here was an actual opportunity to combine his poetry with visual art — the chance for a literal realization of the correspondence among the arts. Méryon, however, responded to Baudelaire's suggestion by insisting on a very literal text. Baudelaire wrote sarcastically to a friend that Méryon would have him write something like, "On the right we have this, on the left that." Méryon, who Baudelaire reported was absently staring at the ceiling as he spoke to him, may have feared that his etchings would be upstaged by Baudelaire's verses, or he may have wanted to include some of his own poems with them instead, as he later did. Or, as Baudelaire believed, he may just have been mad: "A cruel demon has touched the brain of M. Méryon; a mysterious madness has deranged those faculties which seemed as robust as they were brilliant."[11] In another letter he pondered, "After he [Méryon] left me, I wondered how it was that I, who have always had the mind and the nerves, everything necessary, really, to go mad, have never actually done so."[12]

No matter what he thought about the man, there can be no doubt that Baudelaire had an extraordinary regard for Méryon's talent, especially for his power to evoke the city. Having been refused the opportunity to accompany the etchings with his poems, he seemed determined to do them whatever justice he could in his prose:

I have rarely seen the natural solemnity of an

immense city more poetically reproduced. Those majestic accumulations of stone; those spires "whose fingers point to heaven"; those obelisks of industry, spewing forth their conglomerations of smoke against the firmament; those prodigies of scaffolding round buildings under repair, applying their openwork architecture, so paradoxically beautiful, upon architecture's solid body; that tumultuous sky, charged with anger and spite; those limitless perspectives, only increased by the thought of all the drama they contain — he forgot not one of the complex elements which go to make up the painful and glorious décor of civilization.[13]

In a letter to Victor Hugo Baudelaire compared Méryon's work to a passage from Hugo's collection of poems *Les Voix intérieures (Interior Voices)*, in which the older poet described Paris as a "city that a storm has darkened." In the same letter, Baudelaire poignantly, if subconsciously, acknowledges his affinity with Méryon when he recalls that this artist-sailor "had one day bid fare-

Les plus riches cités, les plus grands paysages,
Jamais ne contenaient l'attrait mysterieux
De ceux que le hasard fait avec les nuages.

From "Le Voyage"

The richest cities, the grandest landscapes,
never contain the mysterious attraction
of those formed by chance among the clouds.

From "The Voyage"

Dans le suaire des nuages
Je découvre un cadavre cher,
Et sur les celestes rivages
Je bâtis de grands sarcophages.

From "Alchimie de la douleur"

In the winding sheet of the clouds
I discover the cadaver of a beloved,
and on the celestial shores
I build grand sepulchres.

From "Alchemy of Grief"

59 Edouard Manet
At the Window, 1875

Fascinating correspondences appear in this lithograph by Manet. Some seven years after Baudelaire's death, Manet illustrated Stéphane Mallarmé's translation of Edgar Allan Poe's "Raven," and the man overlooking the city from his window represents the speaker in that poem. Yet the figure corresponds as well to the speaker in "Paysage," for Manet knew well how much his friend felt akin to the American poet. Indeed, it was Baudelaire's marvelous translations of Poe that were responsible for Poe's reputation in France. Baudelaire considered Poe his spiritual twin; in a letter he wrote, "Do you know why I translated Poe? Because he resembled me. The first time I opened a book of his, I saw, with fear and delight, not only subjects I had dreamed of myself, but phrases I had thought of, and which he had written twenty years before."[17]

well to the solemn ocean in order to paint the black majesty of the most disquieting of capitals."[14] The artist also tacitly acknowledged the uncanny sympathy that existed between him and the poet. In a letter to Baudelaire that accompanied his gift of a set of *Eaux-Fortes sur Paris,* he wrote with piteous nostalgia, "I myself, who made them at an epoch, it is true, when my heart was still taken by sudden aspirations toward a happiness which I believed I could attain, look over some of these pieces with a veritable pleasure. They may, then, produce nearly the same effect upon you who also love to dream."[15]

Some of the poems in the new section of *Les Fleurs du mal,* "Tableaux parisiens," share a number of images with Méryon's pictures. For example, "Paysage" ("Landscape"; see PAGE 91), the opening poem of the chapter, finds the poet in his garret contemplating Paris below and beyond. Baudelaire has positioned himself by his high window, "les deux mains au menton" ("my two hands under my chin"), a pose that resembles Méryon's *Stryge* (gargoyle), who peers out over Paris from his perch high atop Notre-Dame (FIG. 57). When Méryon first published the etching in 1854 he called it *La Vigie (The Lookout),* as if the gargoyle were perched on a ship instead of a cathedral. That image relates to Baudelaire's metaphor "ces mâts de la cité" ("these masts of the city") as well as to the tropical seascape imagery found at the climax of the poem. But Méryon also considered his *Stryge* to be the personification of the Luxuria, or lust, that permeates the city. His own verse, which appears in the fourth state of the etching, reads, "Insatiable vampire, / Eternal Luxuria / Coveting the Great City / As its feeding place."[16] Had Méryon allowed Baudelaire to compose verses to accompany his pictures, he would have gotten similar ideas, but far superior poetry.

In "Paysage," Baudelaire demonstrates the love for dreaming Méryon attributed to him when

60 Paul Gauguin
The Sacred Mountain
(Parahi Te Marae), 1892

In *Parahi Te Marae* Gauguin portrays the seductive landscape envisioned by Baudelaire in "Paysage" as an escape from the modern city while he taints it with the skulls that appear on the fence in the foreground. The scene is thus characteristic of Baudelairean duality. Charles Morice writes in his introduction to Gauguin's Tahiti journal, *Noa Noa,* that it is a picture that combines "horror and sublimity." *Parahi Te Marae* is, at least in part, Gauguin's response to Baudelaire's behest to the traveler in "Le Voyage": "Tell me, what have you seen!" which the painter quotes in *Noa Noa.*

61 Edouard Manet
Man Writing in a Café,
c. 1878

he retreats from his Stryge's-eye view of the wintry city and conjures up a tropical landscape. He and Méryon, having sailed in southern seas, both evoke the light-filled tropics in their work, images that stand in sharp contrast to those of the city where dark shadows dominate. "Paysage" is not just a voyage into an urban landscape but ventures as well into a tropical dreamscape in search of relief from the debilitating attractions of urban civilization and its discontents — a motif that also found its place in the works of painters of subsequent generations such as Gauguin and Matisse (see FIG. 60 and "Voyage into the Dream").

Crowds: Guys, Manet, Munch, Ensor

The material for the human drama in Baudelaire's city poems comes as much from his wanderings amid the crowds as from his voyages into his own soul. His city poems in both *Les Fleurs du mal* and *Le Spleen de Paris* derive their shadowy energy from the tension between these sources. The poet first ponders life in the urban maelstrom while he is tucked away in his garret and then makes anxious forays into the city's tumult. The twisting, swarming streets of Paris, snaking their way like arteries and veins through a body, are not only his route into the town and back but are where he finds his subjects, his words, and even the places

RUE DES CHANTRES

Chez ROUHOUX Quai de l'Horloge 29   PARIS. MDCCCLXII   Pierron Imp. r. Marguerin 3

to weave them into allegory. He wrote sitting in a café "in the midst of noise, card games and billiards, so as to be calmer and able to think more clearly" (FIG. 61).[18] He found his images while "crossing the boulevard in great haste, leaping through the mud and across the moving chaos where death arrives from every side at once" (FIG. 80) and "wandering in the gutter with the sad voice of a shivering Phantom."[19] In his early years, when he lived in the Latin Quarter or on the Ile Saint-Louis, his friends reported that he composed poems as he walked through the streets. Much later he stated that the basis for his language in *Le Spleen de Paris* derived "above all from frequenting enormous cities, from the crossroads of their innumerable interrelations" (1:276). In "Le Soleil" ("The Sun") he travels into the city not only "to extract beauty from evil," as he once said, but to excavate his raw material from the streets themselves:

> Je vais m'exercer seul à ma fantasque escrime,
> Flairant dans tous les coins les hasards de la rime,
> Trébuchant sur les mots comme sur les pavés,
> Heurtant parfois des vers depuis longtemps rêvés.

> I go out to practice alone my strange duel, scenting in every corner the chance of a rhyme, stumbling on words like paving stones, colliding sometimes with lines dreamed of long ago.

For Romantics like Delacroix, nature was "un vaste dictionnaire" from which to select the components of art. For Baudelaire the vast dictionary was modern life, and at its center was the city.

> Un matin, cependant que dans la triste rue
> Les maisons, dont la brume allongeait la hauteur,
> Simulaient les deux quais d'une rivière accrue.
>
> From "Les Sept Vieillards"

> One morning, in the melancholy street,
> the houses, stretched upward by the mists,
> looked like the two banks of a rising river.
>
> From "Seven Old Men"

62 Charles Méryon
The Street of Cantors, 1862

63 Félix Buhot
Winter Morning along the Quays, 1883

O fins d'automne, hivers, printemps trempés de boue,
Endormeuses saisons! je vous aime et vous loue
D'envelopper ainsi mon cœur et mon cerveau
D'un linceul vaporeux et d'un vague tombeau.

From "Brumes et pluies"

O end of autumn, winters and springs drowned in mud —
beguiling seasons! I love and praise you for wrapping my
heart and brain in a vaporous shroud — my misty tomb.

From "Mists and Rains"

A UNE PASSANTE

La rue assourdissante autour de moi hurlait.
Longue, mince, en grand deuil, douleur
    majestueuse,
Une femme passa, d'une main fastueuse
soulevant, balançant le feston et l'ourlet;

Agile et noble, avec sa jambe de statue.
Moi, je buvais, crispé comme un extravagant,
Dans son œil, ciel livide où germe l'ouragan,
La douceur qui fascine et le plaisir qui tue.

Un éclair . . . puis la nuit! — Fugitive beauté
Dont le regard m'a fait soudainement renaître,
Ne te verrai-je plus que dans l'éternité?

Ailleurs, bien loin d'ici! trop tard! *jamais* peut-être!
Car j'ignore où tu fuis, tu ne sais où je vais,
O toi que j'eusse aimée, ô toi qui le savais!

TO A WOMAN WHO PASSES BY

The deafening street roared around me.
Tall, slim, and majestic in her mourning garb and grief,
a woman passed, agile and noble,
with statuesque form and luxurious hand,

raising and swinging her scalloped hem.
I, like a wild man, heart palpitating, drank
from her eye, a livid sky where hurricanes are born,
the sweetness that captivates and the pleasure that kills.

One flash . . . then the night! Fugitive beauty,
whose look has suddenly given me new life,
shall I not see you again in all eternity?

Elsewhere! far from here! Too late, never perhaps!
Where you flee, I don't know; where I go, you don't know.
O you whom I might have loved; O you who knew it!

64 Pierre Bonnard
The Square at Evening,
1899

Baudelaire's life in Paris was colored by ambivalence. At times being part of a crowd was efficacious; at others, his greatest need was for solitude. The most poignant encounters with other human beings were fleeting and combined immersion in the crowd with a simultaneous isolation. In his poem "A une passante" ("To a Woman Who Passes By"), a woman glides through the deafening street noise roaring around him: "Un éclair . . . puis la nuit! — Fugitive beauté / Dont le regard m'a fait soudainement renaître, / Ne te verrai-je plus que dans l'éternité?" ("One flash . . . then the night! Fugitive beauty, whose look has suddenly given me new life, shall I not see you again in all eternity?") (See FIG. 64.) Like the poet, the woman, a widow, is also alone. Ironically, the anonymous energy of the city pushes people together as it sweeps them apart, precluding love or permanent relationships.[20]

For the prospective lover the crowd is a setting destined to produce frustration and an ironic isolation, but for the poet and artist, it is a source pregnant with creative possibilities: "Il n'est pas donné à chacun de prendre un bain de multitude: jouir de la foule est un art; et celui-là seul peut faire, aux dépens du genre humain, une ribote de vitalité, à qui une fée a insufflé dans son berceau le goût du travestissement et du masque, la haine du domicile et la passion du voyage. Multitude, solitude: termes égaux et convertibles pour le

65 Constantin Guys, *Les Champs-Elysées,* undated

poète actif et fécond" (1:291; "It is not everyone who can take a bath of the multitude: enjoying the crowd is an art; and only he can relish this debauch of vitality at the expense of the human race who has had a fairy breathe into him in the cradle a hatred of home and a passion for the voyage. Multitude, solitude: terms equal and interchangeable for the active and fertile poet"). This ambivalent attitude toward the crowd is poignantly revealed in the city paintings of artists who were part of the same milieu. Despite the disappointments lurking there, the crowd was,

Baudelaire believed, the place where the modern painter must be, the locus in which he must pursue his art.

Baudelaire enunciated this requirement in the seminal essay "Le Peintre de la vie moderne," which he wrote in 1859–1860, although it was not published until 1863. The delay, in fact, created one of the more interesting ironies in art history. His selection of Constantin Guys (1802–1892), a relatively minor artist, for the title role in this essay, which has come to be regarded as one of the primary documents establishing the criteria for

66 Edouard Manet
Concert in the Tuileries Gardens, 1862

67 Edouard Manet
Charles Baudelaire in Profile Wearing a Hat, 1862

68 Edouard Manet
Concert in the Tuileries Gardens, 1862, detail

Note in this detail how the figure representing Baudelaire (speaking to the poet Théophile Gautier, to whom he dedicated *Les Fleurs du mal*) corresponds closely to Manet's etched portrait of the poet from the same year (FIG. 67).

modernity in art, has always seemed peculiar, because the artist who truly was the painter of modern life as well as the first truly modern painter, Edouard Manet, was one of Baudelaire's closest friends. When the essay was written, however, Manet had not yet produced any significant modern paintings nor had he yet developed his friendship with the poet. So while Baudelaire knew exactly *what* the painter of modern life was when he wrote the essay, the right painter had not yet arrived on the scene. As Guys came closest to fulfilling his conception, he was chosen. By the time the article appeared, Manet had painted *Concert in the Tuileries Gardens* (FIGS. 66, 68), a painting often regarded as a prototypical modern work, and was in the process of becoming the painter Baudelaire envisioned. But because Baudelaire's advancing illness and other pressures in his life had essentially ended his career as an art critic, with the exception of a notice or two, he never properly acknowledged his friend's achievement.[21] Nor did he live to see Manet fulfill the role completely.

Concert in the Tuileries has the "essential quality of presentness" Baudelaire called for, and it fulfills Baudelaire's prescription for works that "extract from fashion whatever element it may

contain of poetry within history [and] distill the eternal from the transitory."[22] It depicts a crowd of stylish Parisians, among whom are many prominent artists, writers, and composers (including Baudelaire and Manet himself), gathered to hear a concert in the park. Given the nature of the poet's relationship with the painter at the time, Baudelaire may very well have suggested the subject to Manet. In the early 1860s Manet and Baudelaire were constant companions and often went together to the Tuileries Gardens, where Manet would sketch "the children playing beneath the trees and the groups of nurses who had collapsed onto the chairs" (FIG. 73).[23] Though Manet's lifelong friend Antonin Proust claims Manet influenced Baudelaire's way of seeing and judging rather than the other way around, the evidence of "Le Peintre de la vie moderne" suggests that Baudelaire had already formed ideas about seeking out such quotidian subjects. The poet and the painter must have discussed these ideas during their walks or over afternoon meals at their favorite cafés. Even more striking is that Manet's painting bears a strong resemblance in composition and feeling to a number of drawings by Guys, especially *The Champs-Elysées,* which Baudelaire owned (FIG. 65).[24]

That Manet has cast himself in *Concert in the Tuileries* as the artist who was, in Baudelaire's words, "spiritually in the condition" of the man of the crowd affirms both the modernism of the work and its tie to the poet-critic. It is as if by means of this painting Manet wished to send a message to Baudelaire that might have read something like: "Had you just waited a little longer you would have known that *I* am the 'painter of modern life,' *I* am the 'passionate spectator' for whom, in your words, 'it is an immense joy to set up house in the heart of the multitude, amid the ebb and flow of movement, in the midst of the fugitive and the infinite' and whom you have likened 'to a vast mirror as vast as the crowd itself; or to a kaleidescope gifted with consciousness, responding to each one of its movements and reproducing the multiplicity of life and the flickering grace of all the elements of life.'"[25]

Manet was not the only artist who fulfilled Baudelaire's call for a passionate spectator. Edvard Munch, a painter who embarked on the voyage into the depths, also traveled into the city and portrayed vividly another aspect of the poet's "bath of the multitude" — the displacement and despair of the individual in the midst of the crowd (FIGS. 71, 72). Both Munch and Baudelaire struggled in their art with the relationship between the inner self and the outer world. Like modern Hamlets, their characters seem desperate to partake in a communion with those around them but are finally at a loss about how to act. They are modern because they are terrified and paralyzed in the midst of the city where everyone, not just the tragic hero, finds himself in the same predicament. In *Evening on Karl Johann* Munch transformed a street in Christiania into a metaphor for the human condition, just as in his poems Baudelaire transformed Paris. Munch included himself as the silhouetted figure separate from the crowd and also, perhaps, as the top-hatted figure in the center. By means of this double presence he emphasizes his isolation even while surrounded by the multitude. In a passage that seems both a key to the painting and an echo of Baudelaire's "A une passante," Munch writes of waiting for a woman: "And then she finally came . . . Pale in the reflection from the horizon in a black dress that fitted closely around her neck, the full yellow-white neck — He had never seen her as beautiful as now. . . . She greeted him with a soft smile and walked on."[26] Munch uses the dynamics of the crowd to reinforce the fleeting and unstable qualities of modern life just as Baudelaire does.

James Ensor (1860–1949) was also fascinated by crowds. *The Cathedral* (1886), *Entry of Christ into Brussels* (1889), and *Hop-Frog's Revenge* (1898), based on Poe's story, all teem with the vibrant harshness of the crowd in the modern city. Their raw quality reveals the barbarity of city life hidden beneath the more comfortable surface of Manet's *Concert in the Tuileries Gardens*. In Ensor's *Music, rue de Flandre* (1891) tension replaces the relaxed equanimity of Manet's concert in the park. The imagery of his *Death Chasing the Flock of Mortals* (1896) (FIG. 70) corresponds to Baudelaire's "Fourmillante cité, cité pleine de rêves, / Où le spectre en plein jour raccroche le passant!"

69 Edouard Manet
Children in the Tuileries Gardens, c. 1861–1862

Pierre Bonnard (1867–1947), Ernst Ludwig Kirchner (1880–1938), and others until they became one of the hallmarks of early twentieth-century art. These renderings are closer to the darkness Baudelaire recognized at the heart of modernity and expressed in his poetry than is Manet's *Concert in the Tuileries,* which, for all its Baudelairean qualities, is more in tune with the less intimate and personal call for modern subjects voiced in his criticism. Baudelaire's enigmatic statement, "When I have inspired universal horror and disgust I shall have conquered solitude" (1:660), speaks to what he hoped to achieve in his poetry: a recognition of the essence of the dark heart of the human race, especially as revealed in his images of the city. Only when poets and artists have forced acknowledgment from their hypocritical readers or spectators of the equation between life and the city that Baudelaire makes in "A Une heure du matin" ("At One in the Morning"): "Horrible vie! Horrible ville" ("Horrible life! Horrible city!") will the terrifying solitude melt away — replaced by a shared vision of the truth.

70 James Ensor
Death Chasing the Flock of Mortals, 1896

71 Edvard Munch
Anxiety, 1896

("Swarming city, city full of dreams, where the specter, in full daylight, grabs the passerby!") from his nightmarish poem "Les Sept Vieillards" ("Seven Old Men"). Both poem and picture strip the civilized veneer from the urban surface. The protean terrors festering in the mud of the urban street, illuminated by corruption and anxiety as much as by gas or electricity, were defined by Baudelaire and then rendered by Munch, Ensor,

Multitude, solitude: termes égaux et convertibles pour le poète actif et fécond. Qui ne sait pas peupler sa solitude, ne sait pas non plus être seul dans une foule affairée.

Le poète jouit de cet incomparable privilège, qu'il peut à sa guise être lui-même et autrui. Comme ces âmes errantes qui cherchent un corps, il entre, quand il veut, dans le personnage de chacun. Pour lui seul, tout est vacant; et si de certaines places paraissent lui être fermées, c'est qu'à ses yeux elles ne valent pas la peine d'être visitées.

Le promeneur solitaire et pensif tire une singulière ivresse de cette universelle communion.

From "Les Foules"

Multitude, solitude: terms equal and interchangeable for the active and fertile poet. He who does not know how to populate his solitude does not know how to be alone in a busy crowd.

The poet enjoys this incomparable privilege of being, as he wishes, himself or another. Like those wandering souls who search for a body, he enters anyone he wants, when he wants. For him alone all is vacant; and if certain places seem to be closed to him, it is because in his eyes they are not worth the trouble of a visit.

The solitary and pensive stroller takes a singular intoxication from this universal communion.

From "Crowds"

72 Edvard Munch
Evening on Karl Johann,
1892

73 Honoré Daumier
The Soup, 1853–1857

Ragpickers and Old Women: Daumier

Perhaps the artist most in accord with Baudelaire's deeply felt concern for oppressed souls in the modern city was Honoré Daumier. Although Baudelaire praised the artist's popular caricatures of city life, he was more moved by Daumier's darker side. "Look through his works," he wrote, "and you will see parading before your eyes all that a great city contains of living monstrosities, in all their fantastic and thrilling reality."[27] As critic Sarah Symmons comments, "Daumier seems to participate in Baudelaire's ambivalent emotions of excitement and horror as he surveys the

city."[28] The miserable existence of the *chiffonier* (ragpicker) was one that fascinated both men. Baudelaire identified with the displacement, itinerancy, and despair of these rummagers and recognized in them the equivalent of the modern poet, of himself, who sifts through "les débris d'une journée de la capitale" (1:381; "the debris of a day in the capital city") for the stuff of his poems. Baudelaire employs his most eloquent and tragic prose describing the perambulations of the ragpicker in the city:

> Everything the great city has rejected, everything it has lost, everything it has scorned and broken, he

collects and catalogues. He consults the archives of debauchery, the shambles of the scrap heap. He makes a triage, an intelligent choice; he picks up, like a miser his treasure, the rubbish, which chewed over by the divinity of industry, will become for him objects of utility or pleasure. Here he is in the somber light of the street lamps tormented by the night wind, going up one of the long, winding streets of little households on Saint-Geneviève hill. For a shawl he wears his wicker basket with its number seven pike. He proceeds, bobbing his head and stumbling on the paving stones, like the young poets who spend all their time wandering in search of rhymes. He talks only to himself; he pours out his soul in the cold air and shadows of the night. It is a monologue so splendid that it makes the most lyrical tragedies seem pitiful.[29]

A copy of Baudelaire's poem "Le Vin des chiffonniers" ("Ragpickers' Wine"), which bears much resemblance to the passage above, was found, in the poet's own hand, among Daumier's papers, and in his visits to the artist's studio, Baudelaire certainly saw Daumier's drawings and paintings of ragpickers, which reveal the same sentiments as those of the poet (FIG. 74).[30]

Baudelaire and Daumier were not only touched by the destitute but also by the working poor, those sufferers who toiled and raised families in conditions of extraordinary deprivation without hope of change for the better. Some of their most memorable poems and paintings contain images of these weary figures moving heavily through the Paris twilight or gaining a moment's solace as they sit down to a frugal repast (FIG. 73).

The plight of older women, especially those with children in tow, also affected both poet and painter. Marcel Proust's comment that "No one has written on the poor with more genuine tenderness than Baudelaire that 'dandy' did"[31] is most poignantly demonstrated in the poet's reflections on the plight of old women who wind their piteous ways through "the sinuous folds" of the city. It is in the poem "Les petites vieilles" ("Little Old Women") that Baudelaire reveals not only their forlorn existences but his own as the solitary man haunting the heart of the city, communing with these women who are lost, momentarily fusing with them in his imagination before withdrawing into his own isolation:

> Mais moi, moi qui de loin tendrement vous surveille,
> L'œil inquiet, fixé sur vos pas incertains,
> Tout comme si j'étais votre père, ô merveille!
> Je goûte à votre insu des plaisirs clandestins:
> . . . .
> Je vous fais chaque soir un solennel adieu!
> Où serez-vous demain, Eves octogénaires,
> Sur qui pèse la griffe effroyable de Dieu?

74 Honoré Daumier
The Beggar, undated

78 Maxime Lalanne, *Demolition for the Creation of the rue des Ecoles,* 1866

Maxime Lalanne's (1827–1886) etchings are one of the most powerful records of the destruction of neighborhoods and displacement of residents carried out by Baron Haussmann and Napoléon III in their relentless zeal to transform Paris.

The "New City": Daumier and Manet

Being lost in the flux of the modern city is also the subject of "Le Cygne" ("The Swan"), one of Baudelaire's greatest city poems, which portrays the confrontation between the longing for the order and stability associated with an ideal past and the inevitable destruction change brings. It is Baudelaire's lament on exile and loss. Specifically, he has in mind the physical changes taking place in the city of Paris and how they have affected his memories.

During the Second Republic (1848–1852) and the Second Empire (1852–1870), Baron Georges Haussmann, Napoléon III's prefect of the Seine, executed a large-scale urban redevelopment of Paris. Ostensibly, the renovations were undertaken to cope with the overcrowding caused by the exploding population, to combat public health problems resulting from antiquated sewage systems, and to remove an enormous number of decrepit, unsafe buildings. But political and economic motives also played a role. The rapidly expanding commercial class needed space in which to build its new residences as well as wide boulevards and parks in which to promenade. The removal of the vast and unsightly slums would at once provide room for these leisure-class amenities and remove eyesores offensive to the upwardly mobile bourgeoisie. Not least among the government's motives was to create wide avenues that would replace many of those narrow streets across which barricades had been so easily built during moments of revolutionary fervor. It is not difficult to understand the enthusiasm for such changes in a regime that harked to the phrase enrichissez-vous (enrich yourself). The order of the day was sophisticated greed, a reverence for wealth for its own sake. Its pursuit, however, especially in the tearing down and ripping up, often followed an unforgiving course. Many old buildings of the kind that Méryon had preserved in his etchings gave way to the onslaught so that, as Baudelaire wrote to his mother in 1860, "the poetic points of view of Paris as they were before the immense demolitions and renovations ordered by the Emperor"[32] were lost. Indeed, the house in which Baudelaire himself was born was torn down to provide access for the boulevard Saint-Germain.[33]

After the boulevards were in place, the idea that they would make life more agreeable for the poor proved a sham. Thousands were simply made homeless. Baudelaire treated this pathetic state of affairs in his prose poem "Les Yeux des pauvres" ("The Eyes of the Poor"). A young bourgeois couple, sitting in a gilded new café on "un boulevard neuf, encore tout plein de gravois et montrant déja glorieusement ses splendeurs inachevées" ("a new boulevard still littered with debris and already showing off its unfinished splendors"), is confronted by a poor family whose eyes reveal the gulf that separated the classes:

LE CYGNE

À Victor Hugo.

1

Andromaque, je pense à vous! Ce petit fleuve,
Pauvre et triste miroir où jadis resplendit
L'immense majesté de vos douleurs de veuve,
Ce Simoïs menteur qui par vos pleurs grandit,

A fécondé soudain ma mémoire fertile,
Comme je traversais le nouveau Carrousel.
Le vieux Paris n'est plus (la forme d'une ville
Change plus vite, hélas! que le cœur d'un mortel);

Je ne voix qu'en esprit tout ce camp de baraques,
Ces tas de chapiteaux ébauchés et de fûts,
Les herbes, les gros blocs verdis par l'eau des
    flaques,
Et, brillant aux carreaux, le bric-à-brac confus.

THE SWAN

To Victor Hugo.

1

Andromache, I think of you! This humble stream,
sad mirror which in days gone by reflected
the immense majesty of your widow's grief,
this false Simois deepened by your tears,

has suddenly moistened a seed in my fertile memory
as I cross the new Carrousel.
Old Paris is no more (the form of a city
changes more quickly, alas! than the heart of a mortal).

Only in my mind's eye can I see the camp of huts,
the piles of roughed out columns and capitals,
the slabs of stone amid the grass become mossy from
    the damp,
and the gleaming tiles amid a chaos of bric-a-brac.

Là s'étalait jadis une ménagerie;
Là je vis, un matin, à l'heure où sous les cieux
Froids et clairs le Travail s'éveille, où la voirie
Pousse un sombre ouragan dans l'air silencieux,

Un cygne qui s'était évadé de sa cage,
Et, de ses pieds palmés frottant le pavé sec,
Sur le sol raboteux traînait son blanc plumage.
Près d'un ruisseau sans eau la bête ouvrant le bec

Baignait nerveusement ses ailes dans la poudre,
Et disait, le cœur plein de son beau lac natal:
"Eau, quand donc pleuvras-tu? quand tonneras-tu,
        foudre?"
Je vois ce malheureux, mythe étrange et fatal,

Vers le ciel quelquefois, comme l'homme d'Ovide,
Vers le ciel ironique et cruellement bleu,
Sur son cou convulsif tendant sa tête avide,
Comme s'il adressait des reproches à Dieu!

2

Paris change! mais rien dans ma mélancolie
N'a bougé! palais neufs, échafaudages, blocs,
Vieux faubourgs, tout pour moi devient allégorie,
Et mes chers souvenirs sont plus lourds que des rocs.

Aussi devant ce Louvre une image m'opprime:
Je pense à mon grand cygne, avec ses gestes fous,
Comme les exilés, ridicule et sublime,
Et rongé d'un désir sans trêve! et puis à vous,

Andromaque, des bras d'un grand époux tombée,
Vil bétail, sous la main du superbe Pyrrhus,
Auprès d'un tombeau vide en extase courbée;
Veuve d'Hector, hélas! et femme d'Hélénus!

Je pense à la négresse, amaigrie et phthisique,
Piétinant dans la boue, et cherchant, l'œil hagard,
Les cocotiers absents de la superbe Afrique
Derrière la muraille immense du brouillard;

A quiconque a perdu ce qui ne se retrouve
Jamais, jamais! a ceux qui s'abreuvent de pleurs
Et tettent la Douleur comme une bonne louve!
Aux maigres orphelins séchant comme des fleurs!

Ainsi dans la forêt où mon esprit s'exile
Un vieux Souvenir sonne à plein souffle du cor!
Je pense aux matelots oubliés dans une île,
Aux captifs, aux vaincus! . . . à bien d'autres encor!

In years past, spread out over this place was a menagerie;
there I saw one morning, at that hour when under
cold and clear skies work begins, when the sweepers
stir a storm of dust into the silent air,

a swan that had escaped from its cage,
scraping its webbed feet over the dry paving stones,
dragging its white plumes over the ragged ground.
Beside a parched streambed, the creature anxiously

bathed its wings in the dust, and heartsick
for its lovely native lake, opened its beak as if to say,
"Rain, when will you pour down? Thunder, when will
        you flash?"
I can still see this forlorn creature,

a strange and fatal myth, like Ovid's man,
his eager head on a contorted neck
twisting toward the sky, the cruel and ironic blue,
as if addressing his reproaches to God.

2

Paris changes! But nothing in my melancholy has stirred!
New palaces and scaffolds, new blocks
and old neighborhoods — all for me become allegory,
and my dear memories heavier than rocks.

Here before the Louvre another image weighs down on me.
I think of my great swan with his tormented gestures,
like all exiles, ridiculous yet sublime,
gnawed at by never-ending desires! And then of you,

Andromache, taken from the arms of a magnificent spouse;
become vile chattel under the hand of proud Pyrrhus;
bowed down in ecstasy before an empty tomb;
widow of Hector, alas; and wife of Helenus!

I think of the negress, emaciated and tubercular,
scuffling in the mud, searching with haggard eye
for the absent palm trees of her superb Africa,
hidden from her by an immense wall of fog.

I think of whoever has lost what can never be found
— ever again! of all who drink tears
and suckle sorrow as did the kindly wolf;
of the frail orphans withering like flowers!

Thus in the forest of my soul's exile,
an old memory has sounded a trumpet call;
and I think of sailors lost on an isle,
of captives, of the vanquished . . . and oh, of so many more!

79 Henri Matisse
The Swan, 1931

Matisse drew a series of swans in preparation for his illustration of Stéphane Mallarmé's "swan" sonnet. This poem, which echoes Baudelaire's "Le Cygne," appears in the same volume as the tribute to Baudelaire that Matisse illustrated with his famous portrait of the older poet (FIG. 49). In this portrait, the artist included the diminutive figure of a swan, as if to affirm the links in the chain that connects Baudelaire, Mallarmé, and himself.

Imp. Bertauts, Paris.

80 Honoré Daumier
The New Paris, 1862

Comme c'est heureux pour les gens pressés, qu'on ait élargi les voies de communication!!!.

"Les yeux du père disaient: 'Que c'est beau! que c'est beau! on dirait que tout l'or du pauvre monde est venu se porter sur ces murs.' — Les yeux du petit garçon: 'Que c'est beau! que c'est beau! mais c'est une maison où peuvent seuls entrer les gens qui ne sont pas comme nous.'" ("The eyes of the father were saying: 'How beautiful! How beautiful! One might say that all the gold of the poor world has flown to these walls.' — The eyes of the little boy: 'How beautiful! How beautiful! but it is a house where only people not like us go in'").

In "Le Cygne" Baudelaire goes beyond the displacement of a particular class to focus on the loss of something more personal. "What mattered for me [in writing 'Le Cygne']," said Baudelaire in a letter to Victor Hugo, "was to express quickly all the suggestions sparked off by an accident, an image, toward all those who love, who are absent, who suffer, toward all those deprived of something they will never find again."[34] The accident to which Baudelaire refers was once seeing a swan that had escaped from its cage in a menagerie scuffling on the dry paving stones of a dusty Paris square. He remembered this incident while he was crossing the newly built Carrousel, the courtyard created by additions to the Louvre. The Carrousel had supplanted the rough-and-tumble slums where the menagerie had existed, and it symbolized the changes that were taking place throughout the city. "Le vieux Paris n'est plus" ("Old Paris is no more"), Baudelaire writes in the poem. The memory of the swan, so out of place, so far from its "beau lac natal," the beautiful lake where it was born, leads Baudelaire to contemplate an aggregation of images that he weaves into a tapestry of displacement and exile: Hugo (to whom the poem is dedicated), the great poet deprived of his home and country; Andromache, the widow of Hector, who lost both husband and homeland;[35] a black woman, struggling, like the

swan, in the Paris streets, separated forever from the coco palms of her superb Africa; Ovid's newly created man pondering his fate in a just-formed world;[36] orphans withering away like drying flowers; mariners forgotten on an isle. "Tout pour moi devient allegorie" ("everything for me becomes allegory"), Baudelaire observes. Together these images, which have both personal associations and universality, represent the estrangement he feels in his life and in life in general. The examples range in time from the Trojan War to the present and thus evoke the cumulative melancholy of the human race.

Daumier was also interested in the dislocation wrought upon the people of Paris by a government bent on completing projects with no concern for the human cost. Haussmann's destruction of the old Paris in order to create the new was the subject of several Daumier lithographs just after the appearance of "Le Cygne." One of the most scathing political satirists of the 1830s, Daumier had by this time turned to a more benign form of satire because he had been jailed for his assaults on the regime of Louis-Philippe and because in the early years of the Second Empire direct criticism of the government and its policies was still risky. As a result Daumier expressed his views through allusion and indirection and focused on the human comedy. In one lithograph a couple is shooed from their bed by workmen who peer through the window and announce that the house is about to be torn down. The caption reads, "Come on, Citizens, get out quickly, it's your turn, we've got to demolish you."[37] In another, a character looks at the site where his domicile formerly stood and says, "But surely this is where I live . . . and I cannot even find my wife." In Daumier's best lithograph on the subject, The New Paris, the figures range from consternated to lost as they try to navigate the width of the new avenues (FIG. 80). A hunched woman with her small child evinces a tentative posture that speaks volumes about the burden of displacement and change on human souls. It is as if Daumier is presenting a comic and visual version of Baudelaire's images and themes in "Le Cygne." People on the rue de Rivoli are surrounded by the dust and rubble, just like the swan on what had become the new Carrousel. The man who can find neither house nor wife is not unlike Andromache removed from Troy and mourning at the empty tomb of her husband. Baudelaire and Daumier, kindred spirits in so much of their art, here

81 Edouard Manet
The Absinthe Drinker, 1860

look at Paris changing and respond with a poem and drawings radically different in approach but surprisingly similar in character and intent.

Manet, more commonly known for depicting the pleasures of Paris, also echoes Baudelaire's themes in "Le Cygne." In the early 1860s, at the time he was painting scenes in the Tuileries gardens under Baudelaire's influence, he also turned his attention to the waifs and wanderers of Paris. Although the two men were superficially different, they had, according to Manet's biographer, Henri Perruchot, "a curiously profound identity of spirit."[38] That led, in the view of Paul Valéry, to a similarity in their choice of subjects: "We need only glance through the slender collection of *Les Fleurs du mal,* noting the significant and as it were concentrated variety of subjects in the poems, and compare it with the variety of subjects to be remarked in the list of Manet's works, to decide on a reasonably obvious affinity between the preoccupations of the poet and the painter."[39] Among those preoccupations was the theme of "Le Cygne," the exiled and detached products of a city in flux.

In the year following the publication of the poem, Manet painted his monumental canvas *Le Vieux Musicien (The Old Musician)* (FIG. 82). Five figures surround an old itinerant violinist in a nondescript but seemingly rural landscape that is most likely near Manet's studio, which was located in a relatively undeveloped section of the city. Qualities that unify the group include a sense of melancholy and an estrangement from their surroundings. And yet, like the members of the band of exiles that Baudelaire assembled in "Le Cygne," each seems alone.

The man in the top hat is easily identifiable as the character in another Manet work, *The Absinthe Drinker,* done several years earlier (FIG. 81).[40] If, as several critics have suggested,[41] Manet's figure of the absinthe drinker is an emblem of

82 Edouard Manet
The Old Musician, 1862

Baudelaire, then we may assume that he meant the top-hatted figure in *The Old Musician* to represent Baudelaire as well. This fellow, dressed in a tattered version of the black suit of the dandy, the outfit Baudelaire ennobled as "the necessary garb of our suffering age,"[42] can be read as a dropout from *Concert in the Tuileries Gardens,* a double of those more fashionable Parisian types, but from the other side of the tracks. We have already noted that Manet incorporated a figure of Baudelaire in *Concert in the Tuileries,* and, in fact, *The Old Musician* can be seen as a kind of companion piece to it, showing what could be the same figures but without the trappings that constitute their "fugitive, fleeting beauty." Here they are presented with their souls laid bare, stripped of their finery, exiled from the superficial comfort of the palace gardens, with their vulnerability and

83 Honoré Daumier
Saltimbanque Playing a Drum, c. 1863

has merely wandered from "l'insouciance et le plaisir" of the Tuileries gardens into the fragmented world of "Le Cygne," *The Absinthe Drinker,* and *The Old Musician.*

The old man with the beard at the far right of *The Old Musician* brings to mind the figure of the wandering Jew, symbol of perpetual exile. Urban castoffs, such as Gypsies, street singers, and orphans were common in the works of both Manet and Baudelaire during this period. Manet was known to take walks in an especially poor and dangerous area of Paris called *Petite Pologne* (Little Poland), not far from his studio. It was there he found some of the models he used for *The Old Musician.* The area, described by Eugène Sue as a neighborhood where "there were no streets but alleys, no houses but hovels, no pavements but a thin carpet of mud and manure," was being demolished by the renovators to make way for the new boulevard Malesherbes just before Manet executed his painting and at about the same time Baudelaire wrote his poem.[43]

The characters in the painting — like its models, and like those in the poem — have been exiled from their place in life by the changes occurring in Paris. Three of the figures are children who are like the "orphans withering like flowers" of "Le Cygne." The one just to the left of the musician was posed for by a young boy whom Manet had taken in as a means of helping out his poverty-stricken family. One day Manet returned to his studio to find that the boy had hanged himself from a rafter. Baudelaire recounted the episode in one of his prose poems, "La Corde" ("The Rope"), which he dedicated to Manet. "La Corde," a tale of family estrangement, takes up the themes of exile and separation from *The Old Musician* and "Le Cygne." The displacement caused by temporal events in Paris goes hand in hand with the universal human experiences of separation from one's parents and from the past.

fundamental humanity revealed. By putting Baudelaire in both works, the painter has made the poet the link between the two disparate worlds of Paris as he depicted them in these major paintings. He also acknowledges in them the fundamental duality of his friend's character, because Baudelaire appears equally at home in each. He

Saltimbanques: Manet, Daumier, Picasso, Rouault, Baziotes

In their works Baudelaire and Manet also seem to be making a symbolic equation between the fate of the poor and the fate of the creative artist in a society dominated by a concern for wealth.[44] In fact, at about the same time that Manet was painting *The Old Musician,* Baudelaire was writing "Le Vieux Saltimbanque" ("The Old Street Performer"), a prose poem in which he specifically draws a parallel between himself as a poet and a down-and-out *saltimbanque* — a street performer often dressed as a commedia dell'arte character, such as Harlequin or Pierrot, whom the fickle world no longer wanted.

The figure in *The Old Musician* that relates most directly to the changes being wrought in Paris is, in fact, the boy dressed in the white Pierrot costume. In the nineteenth century the tradition of the commedia dell'arte troupes had been replaced by various groups of itinerant street players and in Paris also by performances at the Théâtre des Funambules, which featured panto-mimes, vaudevilles, and melodramas. After 1830 the theater was especially famous because of its star, the mime Debureau, for whom Baudelaire and others of the arts community had an almost reverential regard. On July 14, 1862, Baron Hauss-mann's wrecking crews tore down the Théâtre des Funambules on the boulevard du Temple. For many avant-garde artists this must have been the equivalent of demolishing Carnegie Hall, except, of course, that the forces of "progress" in this case prevailed. George Mauner has pointed out that everyone who saw *The Old Musician,* with its Pier-rot figure among a group of outcasts, must have been reminded of this event.[45] Manet's Pierrot is the symbolic equivalent of Baudelaire's swan. Both are pure in their whiteness, both are ex-tracted from their natural places and left homeless in the rubble, and both are members of a loosely knit community of performer-artists, vagabonds, and other exiles.

Théophile Gautier claimed to see in the char-acters of the commedia dell'arte a microcosm of the human condition: Pierrot was "pallid, slender, dressed in sad colors, always hungry and always beaten . . . the ancient slave, the modern prole-tarian, the pariah, the passive and disinherited being."[46] Those who performed on the street had the added mystique of the wanderer or outcast. Generally speaking, street performers were distin-guished by caste. The generic name for the lowest group was *saltimbanque* (literally, one who jumps on a bench or other movable platform). The term came to include homeless and wandering acro-bats, jugglers, mountebanks, strong men, clowns, freaks, and so on.[47]

One reason why the *saltimbanques* and clowns began to appear more and more fre-quently in the literature and art of the period was the tendency of artists and writers to identify with them. Wallace Fowlie has noted that it is "strange that the poet, the most secretive, the most per-sonal, of all heroes is able to pass into the char-acterization of the clown," whom he calls "the hero of the most popular of all the arts."[48] But this is not so difficult to understand. The persona of the nineteenth-century artist was more than ever before one that existed outside the establishment. He was either rejected by it or in opposition to it — or both. The image of the artist-bohemian had been forged by such writers as Henri Murger (1822–1861), author of *Scènes de la vie de bohème* (1848). Through their rootlessness the *saltim-banques* were connected to this image. They bore the romantic connotations of being on the one hand free of society's restraints and on the other outcasts and pariahs. Both of these conditions applied to artists and poets as well, and even appealed to their sense of paradox. The clown was a romantic hero for writers like Hugo, Champ-

85 Pablo Picasso
Two Acrobats with a Dog,
1905

and been his main source of support, and must have felt that the world was passing him by.[52] His great watercolors on the subject were most likely done in the 1860s, following this occurrence as well as the publication of Baudelaire's poem in 1861.[53] Even Henry James's commentary on Daumier's *saltimbanques* — "the crowd doesn't come and the battered tumblers, with their furrowed cheeks, go through their pranks in the void. The whole thing is symbolic and full of grimness, imagination and pity"[54] — evokes Baudelaire as much as it does Daumier.

The figure of the clown also runs through the œuvre of Pablo Picasso (1881–1973); in particular, *saltimbanques,* wandering, melancholy, and wraithlike, make a concentrated appearance in his work during the middle of the first decade of the twentieth century. Although there are no direct

links between Picasso's *saltimbanque* images and the poetry of Baudelaire, his pictures evoke lines from Baudelaire's poem "La Muse vénale" ("The Venal Muse"). Interestingly, Picasso associates *saltimbanques* with poets he knew such as André Salmon (1881–1969), Max Jacob (1876–1944), and Guillaume Apollinaire (1880–1918), all of whom wrote about *saltimbanques*. Picasso and Apollinaire exhibit a symbiosis between poem and picture on the subject of the *saltimbanque* reminiscent of that between Daumier and Baudelaire. In his role as critic, Apollinaire commented on an exhibition of Picasso *saltimbanques* in 1905: "More than all the poets, sculptors and other painters, this Spaniard stings us like a sudden chill. His meditations are laid bare in silence."[55] He places Picasso in the tradition of painters who have used this theme as a means of revealing the self.

In works like *The Family of Saltimbanques* and *Two Acrobats with a Dog* (FIG. 85) with their groups of figures looking as lost in a featureless wasteland as the characters in Manet's *The Old Musician,* Picasso's *saltimbanques* suffer alienation, privation, and rootlessness, just as Baudelaire's and Daumier's do. And just as Daumier and Baudelaire did, Picasso, at some level, identified with these figures. In fact, according to Theodore Reff, he gave his own features to at least two *saltimbanques* in his paintings and also gave several of them the faces of his poet friends.[56] Not only does the *saltimbanque* provide a means for artists and poets to reveal something of their inner selves in their art, it appears to be a common symbol that ties poet and painter together, reaffirming the age-old relationship.

A multitude of clowns exists in the œuvre of Georges Rouault, Baudelaire's "brother in spirit," although none of them appears in the more than seventy works that are direct responses to *Les Fleurs du mal.* Yet there is a strong similarity of feeling between Rouault's clown figures and Baudelaire's poetry. Rouault's comment to his friend the poet André Suarès (1868–1948) about the role his clowns play has a Baudelairean flavor: "We are outcasts: my clowns are not so many dispossessed kings; their laughter is familiar to me; it comes close to unleashing the repressed tears that I feel, and it touches upon bitter resignation."[57] Like the *saltimbanques* of Baudelaire, Daumier, and Picasso, Rouault's clowns are often telling self-portraits (FIGS. 86, 87). Rouault's immediate source for his sad clowns is an occurrence strikingly like the one related by Baudelaire in "Le Vieux Saltimbanque," which Rouault knew well. He tells of a Gypsy wagon stopped along a road where a clown sat mending his brightly colored costume: "This contrast between brilliant and scintillating things made to amuse us, and this infinitely sad life, if one looks at it objectively, struck me with real force. I have expanded all of this. I saw clearly that the 'clown' was myself, ourselves, almost all of us."[58] The title of the masterful aquatint, *Who Does Not Paint Himself a Face?,* from the print series entitled *Miserere,* suggests a universal deception: Everyone paints himself; everyone covers himself over; everyone wears a mask.

In his poem "Le Masque," Baudelaire unveils such a deception. The beautiful mask of the statue ceases to elate him because he quickly discovers that "La véritable tête, et la sincère face / Renversée à l'abri de la face qui ment" ("the true head, and the sincere face is hidden in the shadow of the face that lies") (FIG. 26). In the poem Baudelaire is fooled for a moment by the beauty of the face before him, but then sees the real, the splenetic face full of the knowledge that life must continue despite inevitable and irreparable suffering. The sudden reversal is powerful enough to cause the poet to lose his innocence. The effect of Rouault's work is even greater because it does not fool anyone, not even for a second. There is

no pause whatsoever between illusion and reality, no time for innocence. It is immediately clear that the clown's painted face is despairing. The spectator is left with the jarring, instantaneous contrast between what the clown is expected to be and what he is. Rouault's spiritual closeness to Baudelaire is confirmed when it is noted that the despair emanating from this self-portrait finds its

86 Georges Rouault
Who Does Not Paint Himself a Face?, 1923

equivalent in the profound sadness of the figure he drew to illustrate "L'Irréparable" (FIG. 54).

William Baziotes (1912–1963), an American artist associated with the Abstract Expressionists but with distinct Symbolist leanings, extends the tradition of artists who identified with tragic clowns. Baziotes was devoted to the French Symbolist poets, especially Baudelaire, whom he read repeatedly and whose influence is reflected in many of his works. He undoubtedly knew "Le Vieux Saltimbanque" and also admired Picasso's Harlequins; but, according to his friend Ezio Martinelli, he especially identified with Antoine Watteau's (1684–1721) Gilles,[59] the sad and dreamy Pierrot whose diminutive descendant appears in Manet's The Old Musician. Some of Baziotes's watercolors of clowns exhibit this same sad dreaminess, but his untitled painting of a clown from 1938 (FIG. 88) is quite different. The events of the twentieth century have transformed the clown's expression from one of profound sadness into one of unmitigated terror. Rouault's Head of a Tragic Clown of c. 1904 (FIG. 87) is a premonition of what Baziotes brought to completion almost half a century later. The terrifying contrast between expected frivolity and what appears in Rouault's and Baziotes's clown paintings is every bit as stark as the contrast Baudelaire painted between the beauty of his living love and the corpse rotting in the sun in "Une Charogne." Rainer Maria Rilke has noted that in this poem the confrontation with the horrors that modern art cannot afford to evade began. Baziotes felt kinship with Baudelaire precisely because of the poet's dualistic view of humanity and the world. He wrote, "In my type of painting we have horror and something very beautiful,"[60] just as Baudelaire felt from childhood "the horror of life and the ecstasy of life." Saltimbanques can be found on the path of modernism from Baudelaire, its prophet and first practitioner, all the way into its heart in the first half of the twentieth century.

87 Georges Rouault
Head of a Tragic Clown,
c. 1904–1905

Right:
88 William Baziotes
Untitled, 1938

The Poet's Funeral: Manet's Tribute

Baudelaire died on August 31, 1867. He was buried on September 2, an oppressively hot day capped by a thunderstorm that interrupted the eulogies at the graveside in Montparnasse Cemetery. The group of mourners was small. Among them were Théodore de Banville; Baudelaire's closest friend, Charles Asselineau; Manet; the poet Paul Verlaine; and the photographer Nadar. A day after the funeral Manet wrote to Nadar: "You spoke most eloquently in defense of our poor friend Baudelaire yesterday; you are a man of true feeling. I had already been touched by the loving care shown him in your home by you and

89 Edouard Manet
The Funeral, c. 1867

Le cœur content, je suis monté sur la montagne
D'où l'on peut contempler la ville en son ampleur,
Hôpital, lupanars, purgatoire, enfer, bagne,

Où toute énormité fleurit comme une fleur.
Tu sais bien, ô Satan, patron de ma détresse,
Que je n'allais pas là pour répandre un vain pleur;

Mais comme un vieux paillard d'une vieille maîtresse,
Je voulais m'enivrer de l'énorme catin
Dont le charme infernal me rajeunit sans cesse.

From "Epilogue"

The heart content, I have ascended the mountain,
from where one can contemplate the city in its amplitude:
hospital, brothel, purgatory, hell, prison,

where every outrage blossoms like a flower.
You know well, O Satan, patron of my distress,
I did not climb here in order to spill a vain tear;

but as a lurid old man with an ancient mistress,
I wanted to intoxicate myself on this enormous whore
of a city, whose infernal charm renews me perpetually.

From "Epilogue"

your family."[61] For a period of months before he died Baudelaire was partly paralyzed by a stroke and virtually unable to speak. His friends visited him regularly at the Chaillot Clinic in the rue du Dôme. Among them was Manet's sister-in-law, the painter Berthe Morisot, who played for him on the piano his favorite selections from Wagner.[62] Sometimes they took him out for an excursion. After one such visit Nadar wrote to Manet: "Baudelaire is clamoring to see you. Why didn't you come with us and him today? Will you make up for it next Friday? He missed you very much and surprised me when I went to fetch him by shouting to me in a loud voice from the bottom of the garden, 'Manet! Manet!'"[63]

After the funeral, Manet wanted to pay tribute to the poet. He wrote Asselineau: "I believe you are currently planning an edition of the works of Baudelaire? If there is to be a frontispiece portrait to the *Spleen of Paris,* I have a Baudelaire wearing a hat . . . and I have yet another, more substantial image of him, bare-headed. . . . I would very much like to take this on and naturally, in putting myself forward, I would *give* you my plates."[64] The etchings (FIGS. 67, 90) did eventually appear in a short biographical account of Baudelaire by Asselineau.[65] Perhaps still unsatisfied, however, Manet painted the scene at his funeral (FIG. 89).[66]

Manet knew his friend and his friend's art well enough to understand that a picture of his funeral inspired by his poetry would be an extraordinarily appropriate tribute. Manet might have been thinking of any number of poems when he painted *The Funeral,* but most resonant is the poem intended as an epilogue to the 1861 edition of *Les Fleurs du mal* and eventually published after his death as an epilogue to *Le Spleen de Paris.* It is an elegy for himself in which he looks down on Paris as Manet does on the cemetery, with the city as backdrop: "Le cœur content, je suis monté sur la montagne / D'où l'on peut contempler la ville en son ampleur, / Hôpital, lupanar, purgatoire, enfer, bagne, / Où toute énormité fleurit comme une fleur" (1:191; "The heart content, I have ascended the mountain, from where one can contemplate the city in its amplitude, hospital, brothel, purgatory, hell, prison, where every outrage blossoms like a flower").

Baudelaire foreshadows his own funeral and Manet's rendering of it in one of his "Spleen" poems when he writes, "Pluviôse, irrité contre la ville entière, / De son urne à grands flots verse un froid ténébreux / Aux pâles habitants du voisin cimetière / Et la mortalité sur les faubourgs brumeux" ("Stormy February, hostile to the entire city, pours from his urn great waves of dark coldness on the pale inhabitants of the nearby graveyard and mortality on the foggy suburbs"). Though the funeral was in September, it was as if the February of Baudelaire's poem had attended to give to the poet's burial an atmosphere in keeping with his life and work. Manet, recognizing the significance of the visit, painted the tormented skies bearing down upon graveyard and city — which is nevertheless mottled with extraordinary splashes of light — so that the scene is indelibly stamped with the presence of the poet. By thus evoking duality in his painting, Manet illuminates Baudelaire's art even at the dark moment of his death.

In letters to his mother Baudelaire occasionally showed bravado about his chances for artistic immortality. In the confessional of his poetry, he seemed less self-assured. In "Le Guignon" ("Ill-luck"), whose theme is "Art is long and Time is short," he writes, "Loin des sépultures célèbres, / Vers un cimetière isolé, / Mon cœur, comme un tambour voilé, / Va battant des marches funèbres" ("Far from celebrated tombs, toward an isolated cemetery, my heart, like a muffled drum, beats out funeral marches"). Manet could not assure the future of his friend's reputation in literature. Perhaps he knew he wouldn't have to. His painting of Baudelaire's funeral serves, however, as a perfectly fitting tribute to both the man and his poetry. Perhaps this is what Baudelaire wanted him to do when the words "Manet!, Manet!" burst from the confines of his imprisoned mind.

Peint et Gravé par Manet.1865   Imp. A. Salmon.

90 Edouard Manet
Portrait of Baudelaire, 1865

91 James Abbott McNeill Whistler, *Harmony in Blue and Silver: Trouville*, 1865[1]

Grand délice que celui de noyer son regard dans l'immensité du ciel et de la mer! Solitude, silence, incomparable chasteté de l'azur! une petite voile frissonnante à l'horizon, et qui par sa petitesse et son isolement imite mon irrémédiable existence, mélodie monotone de la houle, toutes ces choses pensent par moi, ou je pense par elles (car dans la grandeur de la rêverie, le *moi* se perd vite!)

From ''Le *Confiteor* de l'artiste''

What a great delight it is to drown one's gaze in the immensity of sky and sea! Solitude, silence, incomparable chastity of the azure! A tiny sail quivering on the horizon, so minute and so isolated that it imitates my irremediable existence, monotonous melody of the wave, all these things thinking through me, or I through them (since in the grandeur of reverie the *I* is quickly lost!).

From ''The *Confiteor* of the Artist''

Voyage into the Dream

Childhood for Baudelaire was the focal point of his dreams — and dreams were the springboard for the images of the ideal in his poetry. As Jean-Paul Sartre puts it in his study of the poet's psyche, "Baudelaire never ceased to regret the 'verts paradis des amours enfantines' ["the green paradise of childhood loves"]. He defined genius as 'childhood regained at will.' He believed 'the child sees everything as a novelty; he is always intoxicated."[2] The poet recorded an incident that reflects this intoxication of childhood to which he returned over and over in his imagination and his art.

In 1832, when he was ten years old, Baudelaire traveled with his mother from Paris to join his stepfather, who had been appointed chief of staff of the Seventh Division, in Lyon. In a letter to his half-brother about the journey he wrote: "Day had fallen and I saw a really fine sight, the sunset; that reddish color formed a remarkable contrast with the mountains, which were as blue as the deepest pair of trousers. After I'd put on my little silk bonnet, I stretched out in the back of the coach and it seemed to me that traveling all the time would be a marvelous life for me."[3]

Within this precocious but still childlike description are the seeds of so much of what became defining characteristics of Baudelaire's mind and art. Here is the obviously natural ability to take what is seen and change it easily into what is written. Here is the fascination with color that became the basis for his preference for Delacroix as the great painter of his era, and, in the mention of the silk bonnet, with the texture that plays such an important role in his own art. Here is the attraction to contrasts among the massive elements in nature — sun, mountains, sea, clouds — the only aspects of nature that as an adult attracted him and that he so often used to describe the dualistic character of the human condition. And the simile that compares the color of the mountains to the color of a pair of trousers reveals Baudelaire's preference for the ways of the city over those of nature, as well as his inclination for the style of the dandy, his refined, civilized hero standing forth against decadence and corruption of the spirit. Finally, there is the attraction to the voyage — subtly associated with dreaming because he notices its appeal while donning his sleeping bonnet and stretching out in the back of the coach. In Baudelaire's poetry, voyages toward the ideal are always the product of dream, and perhaps at no other moment in his life was he so close to the ideal as then, journeying in the safety of an enclosed coach with his mother nearby. Perhaps never again would he be as free of the implacable forces of evil, sin, and remorse that would inform the rest of his life and so much of his art.

Dreams of Paris: Baudelaire, Chirico, I. M. Pei

Much of Baudelaire's poetry and, in his view, all good painting evolved from a forging of dream and reality. If the world evolved from a dream, perhaps God's dream, then recreated worlds emerge from the dreams of artists: "A good picture, which is a faithful equivalent of the dream which has begotten it, should be brought into being like a world. Just as the creation as we see it is the result of several creations, in which the preceding ones are always completed by the following, so a harmoniously-conducted picture consists of a series of pictures superimposed on one another, each new layer conferring greater reality upon the dream and raising it by degrees towards perfection."[4] Dream was so important to Baudelaire that in one poem he states emphatically that he would be happy to leave a world "où l'action n'est pas la soeur du rêve" (1:122; "where action is not the sister of dream"). He notes in his journal, anticipating the dream-provoked works of the Symbolists and Surrealists, "One must desire to dream and know how to dream. The evocation of inspiration. A magic art. To begin writing immediately. I reason too much" (1:671–672).

The metaphor that clarifies this process is the gaze at a closed window or the act of closing windows and shutters in order to open up an interior view. "Celui qui regarde du dehors à travers une fenêtre ouverte, ne voit jamais autant de choses que celui qui regarde une fenêtre fermée" ("The one who looks through an open window from the outside never sees as much as the one who looks at a closed window"), Baudelaire wrote in his prose poem "Les Fenêtres" ("Windows"). In "Paysage" he says, "Je fermerai partout portières et volets / Pour bâtir dans la nuit mes féeriques palais" ("I will close my windows, latch my shutters, and build magical realms in the night"). He sees the harsh winter of Paris, closes his shutters, and in his enclosed space travels into a dream where what he saw and felt is transmuted into poetry. Or he descends into the swarming streets, absorbs their essence, and returns to his high attic, where images combine with dream to form art.

The dreams come in several varieties. There are of course the dream images glimpsed on voyages into the depths: "les corbillards de

RÊVE PARISIEN

À Constantin Guys.

1

De ce terrible paysage,
Tel que jamais mortel n'en vit,
Ce matin encore l'image,
Vague et lointaine, me ravit.

Le sommeil est plein de miracles!
Par un caprice singulier,
J'avais banni de ces spectacles
Le végétal irrégulier,

Et, peintre fier de mon génie,
Je savourais dans mon tableau
L'enivrante monotonie
Du métal, du marbre et de l'eau.

Babel d'escaliers et d'arcades,
C'était un palais infini,
Plein de bassins et de cascades
Tombant dans l'or mat ou bruni;

Et des cataractes pesantes,
Comme des rideaux de cristal,
Se suspendaient, éblouissantes,
A des murailles de métal.

PARISIAN DREAM

To Constantin Guys.

1

It is a fantastical landscape
that mortal eye never saw;
this morning the image,
vague and distant, still ravished me.

Sleep is full of miracles!
By a singular caprice,
I had banished from this spectacular vision
all vegetation in its irregularity;

and, painter proud of my genius,
I savored in my picture
the intoxicating monotony
of metal, marble, and water.

A Babel of staircases and arcades
formed an infinite palace,
full of basins and cascades
falling into dull or burnished gold.

Massive cataracts,
like crystal curtains,
were suspended, dazzling,
on walls of metal.

Non d'arbres, mais de colonnades
Les étangs dormants s'entouraient,
Où de gigantesques naïades,
Comme des femmes, se miraient.

Des nappes d'eau s'épanchaient, bleues,
Entre des quais roses et verts,
Pendant des millions de lieues,
Vers les confins de l'univers;

C'étaient des pierres inouïes
Et des flots magiques; c'étaient
D'immenses glaces éblouies
Par tout ce qu'elles reflétaient!

Insouciants et taciturnes,
Des Ganges, dans le firmament,
Versaient le trésor de leurs urnes
Dans des gouffres de diamant.

Architecte de mes féeries,
Je faisais, à ma volonté
Sous un tunnel de pierreries
Passer un océan dompté;

Et tout, même la couleur noire,
Semblait fourbi, clair, irisé;
Le liquide enchâssait sa gloire
Dans le rayon cristallisé.

Nul astre d'ailleurs, nuls vestiges
De soleil, même au bas du ciel,
Pour illuminer ces prodiges,
Qui brillaient d'un feu personnel!

Et sur ces mouvantes merveilles
Planait (terrible nouveauté!
Tout pour l'œil, rien pour les oreilles!)
Un silence d'éternité.

2

En rouvrant mes yeux pleins de flamme
J'ai vu l'horreur de mon taudis,
Et senti, rentrant dans mon âme,
La pointe des soucis maudits;

La pendule aux accents funèbres
Sonnait brutalement midi,
Et le ciel versait des ténèbres
Sur le triste monde engourdi.

Not trees but colonnades
surrounded the sleeping ponds
in which gigantic naiads,
like vain women, stared at their reflections.

Sheets of blue water floated out
from among the quays of rose and green,
coursing toward
the remote borders of the universe;

Stones of unknown origin
lay in magical streams
and immense plates of dazzling glass
reflected everything.

Carefree, silent
Ganges traversed the skies
and poured treasures from their urns
into diamond gulfs.

Architect of my fancy,
I directed at my will
an obedient ocean to pass
through a tunnel studded with gems;

and every color, even black,
took on a clear and iridescent lustre;
the glory of flowing liquid
was fixed in crystallized rays.

No foreign star, no stray
sunbeam, nothing from the sky,
was needed to illuminate these prodigies,
which emitted their own brilliance.

And over these shimmering marvels
hovered (terrible novelty!
all was for the eye; nothing for the ear)
an eternal silence.

2

Waking, my eyes aflame,
I saw the horror of my hovel
and felt the sharp point
of cursed despair reenter my soul.

The clock with deadly accents
brutally sounded noon,
while the sky poured shadows
over the sad, benumbed world.

94 Paul Gauguin
Te Raau Rahi, 1891

«Au bord de la mer, une belle case en bois, enveloppée de tous ces arbres bizarres et luisants dont j'ai oublié les noms ... dans l'atmosphère, une odeur enivrante, indéfinissable ... dans la case un puissant parfum de rose et de musc ... plus loin, derrière notre petit domaine, des bouts de mâts balancés par la houle ... autour de nous, au-delà de la chambre éclairée d'une lumière rose tamisée par les stores. ... »

From ''Les Projets''

''Near the sea, a beautiful wooden hut surrounded by strange shining trees the names of which now evade me ... in the air, an intoxicating, indefinable aroma, a powerful perfume of rose and musk ... farther away behind our little domain, the tips of the masts bobbing on the swells ... around us, pink light softly flowing through the blinds, illuminating our chamber. ... ''

From ''Projects''

resemblance to the image Baudelaire conjured up in the latter poem when he expressed his wish to paint his ideal city with its "enivrante monotonie / Du métal, du marbre et de l'eau" and "d'immenses glaces éblouies / Par tout ce qu'elles reflétaient!" ("intoxicating monotony of metal, marble, and water" and "immense plates of dazzling glass reflect[ing] everything"). It is a further irony that Baudelaire wrote the two poems, one mourning the loss of a remembered Paris and the other creating an imagined one, in the same year (1859).[8]

In a letter to one of his editors Baudelaire defended and explained "Rêve parisien" by tersely stating that "a dream which separates things and breaks them down, creates the new."[9] Pei and Chirico, and in a sense Cubist and Surrealist painters from Picasso and Robert Delaunay (1885–1941) to Joan Miró (1893–1983) have made Baudelaire's Parisian dream come true. They have also testified in work after work to Baudelaire's role as avatar of the modern. Like the speaker of "Rêve parisien," they are all architects of their fantasies.

Of course, the images of lifeless perfection in the first half of the poem constitute an illusion. In the last two stanzas, the poet awakens from his dream. His bubble is pricked, and his soul receives a sharp reminder of the cursed world that still exists. Similarly, Pei's pyramid, with its axes stretching out literally and figuratively to so much of the art of the past, including the sites of Manet's *Concert in the Tuileries Gardens* and Christophe's *La Comédie humaine*[10] down the esplanade, cannot deny by its glistening presence that the surrounding world is any less troubled than the one Baudelaire saw upon awakening from his dream.

Dreams of a Tropical Paradise: Baudelaire, Gauguin, Matisse

The only voyage of any significant duration or distance Baudelaire undertook was the one his stepfather coerced him into taking when he was twenty. He sailed aboard the *Paquebot-des-Mers-du-Sud* bound from Bordeaux to Calcutta. Though he later entertained his friends with evidently made-up stories of derring-do in the interior of India, Baudelaire got only as far as the Indian Ocean islands of Mauritius and Réunion. In spite of the relative brevity of the journey (fewer than eight months from start to finish) and a less than enthusiastic reaction to it at the time, Jean Prévost has noted that it inspired ten times the number of images in his poetry than his previous twenty years of life combined.[11]

His tropical dream emerges in a number of poems that draw their imagery from this southern

95 Paul Gauguin
The Brooding Woman,
1891

voyage. In one, "Les Projets" ("Projects"), while walking in the city, he stops in a print shop and discovers several engravings that induce imaginary journeys. Looking at an engraving of a tropical landscape, he concludes, "c'est *là* qu'il faudrait demeurer pour cultiver le rêve de ma vie" ("it is *there* that I must go to cultivate the dream of my life"). Baudelaire did not, of course, in reality fulfill this dream. At the end of the same poem, after he returns to the solitude of his room, "à cette heure où les conseils de la Sagesse ne sont plus étouffés par les bourdonnements de la vie extérieure" ("at this hour when the counsels of Wisdom are no longer snuffed out by the clamor of outside life"), he asks, "Pourquoi contraindre mon corps à changer de place, puisque mon âme voyage si lestement?" ("Why force my body to change places when my soul travels so easily?"). These passages from "Les Projets" explain much about why a man fascinated by voyages so seldom left Paris. To travel he needed only to look at pictures and dream.

The dream in the poem is, however, later lived out by a voyager-painter whose sentiments were surprisingly similar to Baudelaire's and may have been derived in part from the poet. Paul Gauguin (1848–1903) was determined to leave the torments of modern civilization to cultivate a dream. But although part of his dream was to remove himself from many of the trappings of his cultural milieu, he acknowledged his debt to the art and literature that helped to shape him. In his journal *Avant et Après* he wrote, "I believe the thought which has guided my work, a part of my work, is mysteriously linked with a thousand other thoughts, some of my own, some those of others."[12] In a letter to Odilon Redon in September 1890 about his determination to go to Tahiti, Gauguin insists that although he is finished with the civilized world, he will nevertheless take with him "a whole little world of friends." One "friend" was

96 Paul Gauguin
Nave Nave Fenua (Land of Delight), 1894

Manet, whose *Olympia* he carried to Tahiti in the form of an etching. Another was Redon, some of whose prints he also took. Evidently another was Baudelaire, by whom he was probably notified in advance that no matter where he traveled there would be no escape. In *Noa Noa,* Gauguin's illustrated account of his sojourn in the South Seas, the painter strategically places a line from Baudelaire's poem "Le Voyage," "Dites, qu'avez-vous vu?" ("Tell me, what have you seen?"), at the beginning of the chapter in which he reveals his disillusionment with what he has found. Gauguin's question from the same journal, "Was I to have made this far journey only to find the very thing which I had fled?" is a question entirely parallel to the themes of "Le Voyage." This long poem opens with a child hovering over his maps and prints by the light of his lamp and dreaming of the grand world. As the poem progresses, however, sailors who have seen many exotic and diverse sights convince him that the knowledge they have gained from their voyages is bitter:

> Le monde, monotone et petit, aujourd'hui,
> Hier, demain, toujours, nous fait voir notre image:
> Une oasis d'horreur dans un désert d'ennui!

> The world, small and monotonous, today, yesterday, tomorrow, and always, makes us see our own image: an oasis of horror in a desert of ennui.

The little boy dreaming in the back of the coach or looking at his maps in the safety of his room thinks nothing would be better than always to travel. He has grown up to discover the unpalatable truth, and he has discovered it, ironically, without going much of anyplace. His journey into his own interior has been enough. Gauguin must have recognized himself in "Le Voyage" as "le vieux vagabond, piétinant dans la boue, / Rêve, le nez en l'air, de brillants paradis" ("the old vagabond, trampling in the mud, who dreams, nose in the air, of brilliant paradises"). So many of Gauguin's paintings, like Baudelaire's poems, gain their power from the contrast between color-drenched landscapes and exotic but brooding figures. The sad-faced women almost ubiquitous on his canvases speak silent volumes about the troubles he has discovered in paradise, the same troubles Baudelaire has discovered within. The women's expressions attest to the disparity between the glorious exteriors in which they live and the tormented interiors that fester beneath the surface. They too have seen "Le spectacle ennuyeux de l'immortel péché" ("The despairing spectacle of immortal sin").

Both poet and painter have created idylls untainted by sorrow, but they are few. For Baudelaire "la mer des Ténèbres" ("the sea of shadows") lurks under every sailor's vessel, and for Gauguin the subversive element in a facial expression or body posture marks his œuvre, paradoxical as it may seem, with a somber tone (FIG. 95). Yet it is these hints of darkness in a tropical sea of light that yield the life-giving tension to what might otherwise be little more than extraordinarily painted pretty pictures. Gauguin's statement in *Noa Noa* that "the dream which brought me to Tahiti was brutally disappointed by the actuality"[13] reveals that the dark spirits haunting his pictures have a Baudelairean tint. His sentiment is particularly evident in the famous woodcut *Nave Nave Fenua* in which the meaning of the title, "delightful land," is sharply contradicted by the expression on the face of the native woman and the sinister creatures that prowl the landscape (FIG. 96).

Recollection of a charmed past in a tropical paradise lies at the center of one of Baudelaire's finest poems, "La Vie antérieure" ("A Former Life"). But this sonnet also includes more than a vision of unencumbered bliss, more than a dream of escape to paradise. Its poignancy derives from the contrast between a remembered tropical setting of extraordinary *volupté,* the image of which dominates the poem, and the final couplet, which reveals a residual and irremediable sorrow. Even living "sous de vastes portiques / Que les soleils marin teignaient de mille feux" ("beneath vast porticoes tinted by the thousand fires of marine suns") cannot alleviate the ever-present sorrow in the human soul.

Like Gauguin, Henri Matisse had also traveled to Tahiti, and many works created years after his tropical voyage, like Baudelaire's, reflect the influence of the journey. As noted earlier, Matisse made illustrations for an edition of *Les Fleurs du mal* in the early 1940s. The portrait of the man

97 Henri Matisse
Self-Searching at Midnight
1944

he drew to illustrate "La Vie antérieure" for that same edition was, like the Icarus figures noted earlier, particularly revealing (FIG. 98). The painter's friend, the novelist and poet Louis Aragon, describes the figure in the drawing as an "aging man, bald, bespectacled, thin-lipped, with crumpled collar."[14] Aragon claims he could never read the poem after having seen the portrait and not recall "a colonial official on the point of retirement." Indeed, the image evokes some minor bureaucrat, perhaps of the Bureau of Colonial Affairs, who is daydreaming at a Paris desk, thinking about his golden age in some mostly imagined edenic outpost. In this context the character also brings to mind an older, somewhat less naive version of the child in "Le Voyage," reading his maps and dreaming.

Aragon notes a similarity between this portrait and Matisse's portrait of a young Baudelaire executed for the same volume (FIG. 97). His idea is that the lines Matisse used in the two drawings connote an identity between them, thus signifying that Matisse saw the older man as Baudelaire himself wistfully dreaming of a lost past.[15] One need only recall the author of "Le Cygne" lamenting how life changes faster than "le cœur d'un mortel" ("the heart of a mortal") or the poet of "Spleen" crying, "j'ai plus de souvenirs que si j'avais mille ans" ("I have more memories than if I were a thousand years old") to recognize the appropriateness of Aragon's suggestion in relation to the power of memory for Baudelaire. Yet although Aragon's comparison makes perfect sense, it is equally revealing to compare the portrait for "La Vie antérieure" to a self-portrait by Matisse of the same period (FIG. 99). Once these two portraits are juxtaposed, it is not much of a leap to suggest that Matisse absorbed the poem as an account of himself as well. This was a juncture when his remedy against the difficulties of the time — his health, the war, his separation from his family — was the power of recollection.[16] Even Matisse, who claimed that "what I dream of is an art of balance, of purity and serenity, devoid of troubling or depressing subject matter . . . a soothing, calming influence on the mind, something like a good armchair that provides relaxation from physical fatigue,"[17] was capable of introducing the shadows of life into his so often sunny canvases. As with Gauguin, evidence of this appears throughout his œuvre, most commonly in the troubled expressions on the faces of women who recline in otherwise voluptuous, pleasure-filled settings.

And certainly in this later period, when there were so many difficulties, Matisse depended on

LA VIE ANTÉRIEURE

J'ai longtemps habité sous de vastes portiques
Que les soleils marins teignaient de mille feux,
Et que leurs grands piliers, droits et majestueux,
Rendaient pareils, le soir, aux grottes basaltiques.

Les houles, en roulant les images des cieux,
Mêlaient d'une façon solennelle et mystique
Les tout-puissants accords de leur riche musique
Aux couleurs du couchant reflété par mes yeux.

C'est là que j'ai vécu dans les voluptés calmes,
Au milieu de l'azur, des vagues, des splendeurs
Et des esclaves nus, tout imprégnés d'odeurs,

Qui me rafraîchissaient le front avec des palmes,
Et dont l'unique soin était d'approfondir
Le secret douloureux qui me faisait languir.

A FORMER LIFE

Long ago I lived beneath vast porticoes
tinted by the thousand fires of marine suns;
the evening light on their great pillars, straight and majestic,
transformed them into grottoes of basalt.

The waves, rolling images of the skies,
mingled solemnly and mystically
the powerful harmonies of their rich music
with the colors of the sunset reflected in my eyes.

It was there that I lived in voluptuous calm, ensconced
amid the azure skies, the waves, and the splendors
— tended by naked slaves who, saturated with perfumes,

fanned my forehead with palm fronds,
and whose only care was to search out
the secret sorrow that made me languish.

Left:
98 Henri Matisse
A Former Life, 1944

99 Henri Matisse
Self-Portrait, Three-Quarter View, 1948

100 Henri Matisse
Sadness of the King, 1952

reverie as a means of coping with the darker erup-
tions. "I'm growing old, I delight in the past" and
"I leave the radio playing and live on my memories" were among his recorded comments of the
time.[18] His memory came to play an ever-more
important role in his creative process as the end
of his life drew near. The great works of his last
years — the paper cutouts — are clearly retrospective, conjuring up an idealized past for their

theme.[19] In "La Vie antérieure," Matisse recognized Baudelaire's call to the power of memory
and acknowledged his own current state of mind
by illustrating the poem with a self-portrait.

"La Vie antérieure" as a source of inspiration
for Matisse goes further, however, than this mini-
malist self-portrait. The monumental (9'7" × 13')
and symbolic paper cutout *La Tristesse du roi (Sadness of the King)* of 1952 (FIG. 100) is a dramatic

response to the poem and perhaps his most revealing work during his last years. Pierre Schneider calls *Sadness of the King* Matisse's last self-portrait and says it reads like an illustration of "La Vie antérieure."[20] The work was very important to Matisse. He wrote to Jean Cassou, "Your letter about *Sadness of the King* touches me greatly because it confirms my own opinion about this panel, which I consider equal to all my best paintings."[21] It was filled, the painter continued, with "profound pathos." This makes it stand out from most of the paper cutouts, which radiate pure joy with no hint of sorrow. The work is, as Schneider also points out, like all the paper cutouts, "the fruit of the mnemonic function which removes the aging man willy-nilly from his present circumstances."[22] In this sense, *Sadness of the King* can be interpreted as the complex of images flickering behind the broad forehead of the daydreaming self-portrait he drew for "La Vie antérieure" — an evocation of bittersweet recollections parallel to those in the poem.

Matisse described the work in a letter to the director of the Museum of Modern Art in Paris, where he wanted it to hang. He asks, "Have you seen in my studio a large gouache panel with some figures: a sad king, an engaging dancer, and a character playing a sort of guitar from which fly golden saucers, which circle around the upper part of the composition and end up in mass around the dancer in action?"[23] The speaker of the poem recalls a similar scene. In his dream-memory he is the king of a tropical paradise who lives amid voluptuous calm and is surrounded by naked slaves who fan his brow. As in "Rêve parisien" the poet becomes "a painter proud of his genius" for constructing a utopia. In fact, "La Vie antérieure" is the tropical equivalent of "Rêve parisien." It is a utopia with softer, warmer, more sensual features than the glistening but diamond-hard surfaces of Baudelaire's idealized Paris. And

like "Rêve parisien" it is not a source of pure light. The conclusion of each poem contains a reversal that shrouds paradise in a fog of despair.

In "La Vie antérieure" Baudelaire is, as it were, at his most Matissean. In so many poems his depiction of spleen upstages the presentation of the ideal; the turmoil and despair overwhelm the reader, relegating harmony and tranquillity to a relatively minor role. But here the sumptuous imagery and edenic bliss coat the surface of reality like a soothing balm, and only in the last tercet of the sonnet does darkness tint his tableau. *Sadness of the King* mixes similar elements and produces an analogous effect. In his own way Matisse was responding to Baudelaire's memory of a luxuriant past while managing to include the theme of irreparable sorrow. He has composed the picture so that the diminutive figure of the sad king is finally separate from his voluptuous surroundings and, despite the efforts of his dancer and musician, is unconsolable. Here is the solitary Baudelaire. Even when he travels to the tropical paradise of his lost past, the final image remains the same: he is alone in the midst of the crowd. The painter acknowledges this enduring pain in both the title of the work and the image. Like the old *saltimbanque* of Baudelaire's prose poem and Daumier's drawings, he resigns himself to a final sadness.

Skies and Stillness: Baudelaire and Landscapes of the North

A strong bond between an artist like Matisse, who dwells so often in the realms of light, and a poet like Baudelaire, a confidant of darkness, seems at first unlikely, yet Matisse had a profound understanding of the poet. He was not seduced as were so many of Baudelaire's lesser illustrators by the idea that he was solely a poet of debauchery.[24] As far back as 1904 Matisse took the title for one of his seminal works, *Luxe, Calme et Volupté,* from the refrain of one of Baudelaire's few almost purely idyllic poems "L'Invitation au voyage" ("Invitation to the Voyage") (FIG. 101): "Là, tout n'est qu'ordre et beauté, / Luxe, calme et volupté" ("There, all is order and beauty; luxury, calmness and pleasure." Matisse's painting not only evokes the luxury, calmness, and voluptuous pleasure of Baudelaire's poem, but also in its balanced composition suggests the orderly beauty referred to in the refrain. There is, however, a very significant difference. Matisse's vision is set in a southern landscape, if not a tropical one, on the Côte d'Azur, where the climate is unambiguously receptive. Baudelaire's poem takes place not in the sun-drenched south but under the fog-shrouded skies of the north. In his "Salon de 1846" Baudelaire explains that it is the north, wrapped in mists, that is the source of dreams. "Romanticism is a child of the North. . . . The South, in return, is all for nature; for there nature is so beautiful and bright that nothing is left for

101 Henri Matisse
Luxe, Calme et Volupté,
1904

man to desire, and he can find nothing more beautiful to invent than what he sees."[25]

The inherent mystery of the wet and cloudy north held infinite possibilities for the poetic imagination. "L'Invitation au voyage" emerges out of such a northern dream, born of mystery and indistinctness. Its light is neither bright nor warm but sodden, filtering through cloudy skies. Here is yet another backdrop for a utopian dream different from the azure skies and palm fronds of "La Vie antérieure" or the angular clarity of "Rêve parisien." "L'Invitation au voyage," which exists in both verse and prose versions, is a powerful expression of the ideal as Baudelaire dreamed it.

The verse poem is divided into three stanzas, each presenting an image like a painting and concluding with the famous refrain quoted above. The first stanza, in which the poet addresses a woman who is identified as child and sister and proposes to her a voyage to a land that she resembles, contains a compelling description of a largely shapeless landscape. Its main feature is an expanse of turbulent, cloudy sky suffused with light from misty suns.

Skies such as these always had a powerful effect on Baudelaire. They were, in fact, one of the few aspects of nature that he liked, probably because they seemed to him at once comforting and frightening, an amorphous representation of the duality and ambiguity of his own state of being. Not surprisingly, the skies he saw in paintings and prints made as great (or even greater) an impression on him as those in nature. The cloud-filled skies of Delacroix's *Ovid in Exile among the Scythians* and Méryon's etchings of Paris provoked his imagination by means of their unpredictability: "Les plus riches cités, les plus grands paysages, / Jamais ne contenaient l'attrait mystérieux / De ceux que le hasard fait avec les nuages" (1:131; "The richest cities, the grandest landscapes, never contain the mysterious attraction of those formed

105 Johan Barthold
Jongkind
Frigates, Port of Harfleur,
1863

LE PORT

Un port est un séjour charmant pour une âme fati-
guée des luttes de la vie. L'ampleur du ciel, l'architecture mobile des nuages, les colorations changeantes
de la mer, le scintillement des phares, sont un prisme
merveilleusement propre à amuser les yeux sans
jamais les lasser. Les formes élancées des navires, au
gréement compliqué, auxquels la houle imprime des
oscillations harmonieuses, servent à entretenir dans
l'âme le goût du rythme et de la beauté. Et puis,
surtout, il y a une sorte de plaisir mystérieux et aris-
tocratique pour celui qui n'a plus ni curiosité ni ambition, à contempler, couché dans le belvédère ou
accoudé sur le môle, tous ces mouvements de ceux
qui partent et de ceux qui reviennent, de ceux qui
ont encore la force de vouloir, le désir de voyager ou
de s'enrichir.

THE PORT

A port is a lovely place to rest for a soul tired from the
struggles of life. The immensity of sky, the fluid architecture
of the clouds, the changing colors of the sea, the twinkling
of the beacons are a wonderful prism for amusing the eyes
without ever tiring them. The slender shapes of the ships,
with their complicated rigging, which shift in harmony with
the swells, provide the soul with a taste of rhythm and beauty.
And then, above all, there is a sort of mysterious and aristo-
cratic pleasure for the man who, sequestered in the belvedere
or leaning against the jetty, has neither the ambition nor the
curiosity to watch those who are arriving or leaving or to
contemplate those who still have the energy to yearn, who
have the desire to travel or enrich themselves.

from Sumatra by the merchantmen of the Dutch East India Company. Baudelaire acknowledges in several places his fascination with the world of the Low Countries as a fertile source for dreams and notes that it is indeed from Dutch paintings that his images come. He asks himself in his prose poem "N'importe où hors du monde," "Puisque tu aimes tant le repos, avec le spectacle du mouvement, veux-tu venir habiter la Hollande, cette terre béatifiante? Peut-être te divertiras-tu dans cette contrée dont tu as souvent admiré l'image dans les musées. Que penserais-tu de Rotterdam, toi qui aimes les forêts de mâts, et les navires amarrés au pied des maisons?" ("Since you love your leisure and the spectacle of motion, do you wish to live in Holland, that blessed land? Perhaps you would be diverted in that land you have often admired in images in museums. What do you think of Rotterdam, you who love the forests of masts and the ships anchored at the foot of houses?") In a commentary on Johan Barthold Jongkind (1819–1891), he writes that in his pictures the Dutch painter has "enshrined the secret of his memories and reveries — as calm as the banks of the great rivers and the horizons of his noble country" (FIG. 105).[31]

The third and final stanza of "Invitation to the Voyage," drawing from the painted images of Jongkind and his Dutch predecessors, repaints the ships resting on the quiet canals now bathed in a warm sunset. The poem seems intentionally constructed so that both the first and the third stanzas frame the central stanza between two harmonious landscapes.

The central stanza, which can be read as the equivalent of genre painting — an interior with elements of still life — is given a special position by this framing that reflects the importance of interior space for Baudelaire. Again, Holland is the source here; Baudelaire's interior is an amalgam of Dutch seventeenth-century interiors and still

lifes. Two phenomena stand behind Baudelaire's incorporation of such images in this central stanza and in the corresponding passages of the prose poem. First, a revival of interest in seventeenth-century Dutch painting was being led by a number of art critics Baudelaire knew, including Arsène Houssaye, one of his editors, and Théophile Thoré-Bürger, who expressed his enthusiasm for these works in conversations with Baudelaire as well as in his writings.[32] Second, Baudelaire's long-standing and profound attraction to interior spaces was expressed in all his writings, from letters to art criticism to poetry.

Interior Peace: Baudelaire, Dutch Interiors, Redon's Flowers

For Baudelaire, controlling interior space and keeping order in an inherently chaotic existence were intimately connected. Baudelaire's craving for order — seen in the uniformity of his attire, the obsessive need for perfection in his work, and the symmetry in his poetic structures — was a means of staving off the chaos that he saw at the center of his being. This need for order also served as a bulwark against his bad habits, what he called his "nonchalance," "selfishness," and "those violent bursts of uncouthness, the sorts of things you always find in lives that are disorderly and isolated."[33] The lifelong intensity of his relationship with his mother suggests a need to return to the maternal interior — a place completely protected from the chaos of the outer world — a need finally and symbolically fulfilled by his stay with her in her seaside cottage at Honfleur, a period marked, it should be noted, by a startling burst of creativity.

As explained by Richard D. E. Burton, "Honfleur characterized that 'vrai pays de Cocagne' to which . . . he had imaginatively transported himself in the two versions of 'L'Invitation au Voyage.'" Burton continues that Honfleur was "the embodiment of the Baudelairean ideal of enclosed concentration. . . . Secure, stable and reposeful behind its protective wall, the tiny port opened up to a marine prospect uniquely suited to Baudelaire's taste and needs in that, an 'infini diminutif,' it miraculously united the limitless and the limited."[34] In a letter to his mother written close to the end of his life, he said, "My stay at Honfleur has always been the dearest of my dreams."[35] In Paris after a foray into the chaos of the city he could achieve order and control by returning to his cloistered garret. In his only short story, "Le Fanfarlo," his central character notes that intimate feelings can be experienced only while at leisure in a very narrow space. Baudelaire suggested in a letter to a fellow writer that even the infinite could be usefully contained: "Have you noticed," he wrote, "that a section of the sky through a ventilator or between two chimneys,

106 Emmanuel de Witte
Interior with Woman at the Clavichord, c. 1660

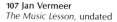
107 Jan Vermeer
The Music Lesson, undated

interiors of the Dutch painters of the seventeenth century also appealed to his craving for order and supplied him with a way of imagining the voluptuous without being led by such thoughts into the depths. The orderliness of these pictures, with their subtle geometricity softened by diffused light and enlivened by a quiet sensuousness, yields a vision of a universe in which the basic elements of life, so conducive to chaos elsewhere, are arranged and presented in a fashion that permits a vision of a harmonious existence. They are capable of sustaining this vision even when the evidence of one's own reality contradicts such a conception at every turn. To a soul like Baudelaire's, tortured by the impossibility of achieving such a beatific state, these pictures must have had enormous appeal. He must have seen in them a means to counteract original sin, repair the irreparable, and reach the ideal. Perhaps this is why he describes Holland as "blessed" and why he recreates a Dutch interior as the centerpiece of "L'Invitation au voyage."

Baudelaire's psychological and spiritual motives for responding to these paintings were evidently not much different from the motives of those who painted them. John Michael Montias writes that "nothing apparently could ruffle the quiet majesty" of the art of Jan Vermeer (1623–1675), art that contains no hints of the chaos of his own domestic circumstances. Montias also makes possible a comparison between the idealized images of Vermeer and those of Baudelaire, and for that matter Matisse, when he notes that Vermeer's images derive from "a sense of recollected tranquillity." This tranquillity, in turn, creates a spirit of mystery achieved through geometry and light that isolates and reveals forms and "endows them with their immutable perfection." "Like Vermeer himself," Montias points out, quoting Baudelaire's "La Beauté," "Beauty abhors 'le movement qui dépare les lignes'" ("the move-

two rocks or through an arcade, gives a more profound idea of the infinite than a great panorama seen from a mountaintop?"[36] Sitting in a cherished spot, the "belvedere," a small watchtower on his mother's property at Honfleur, and regarding the vista of the estuary and channel beyond (FIG. 103), the poet could contemplate the wonder of the infinite while still remaining protected by an ordered interior space. The extraordinary prospect of controlling the abyss may have occurred to him while poised at such a vantage point.[37]

The delicately harmonious and luminous

ment that displaces the lines'').[38] Writing about the only known painting, *Still Life with a Bridle,* of another seventeenth-century Dutch painter, Johannes Torrentius (1589–1644), who like Baudelaire was prosecuted by an intensely bourgeois government for offenses against sexual morality and God, Zbigniew Herbert says, ''As a legacy he left us an allegory of restraint, a work of great discipline, self-knowledge, and order, contradicting his reckless existential experience.''[39]

These paintings themselves are the best evidence of their correspondence with Baudelaire. In Emmanuel de Witte's (1617–1691/92) *Interior with a Woman at the Clavicord* (FIG. 106) one can see the spirit if not exactly the letter of Baudelaire's interior from the prose version of ''L'Invitation au voyage'':

> Les soleils couchants, qui colorent si richement la salle à manger ou le salon, sont tamisés par de belles étoffes ou par ces hautes fenêtres ouvragées que le plomb divise en nombreux compartiments. Les meubles sont vastes, curieux, bizarres, armés de serrures et de secrets comme des âmes raffinées. Les miroirs, les métaux, les étoffes, l'orfèvrerie et la faïence y jouent pour les yeux une symphonie muette et mystérieuse.

> The light of the setting suns, which so richly colors the dining room or the salon, sifts through the beautiful fabric of the curtains or through the lofty windows elaborately divided into leaded glass squares. The enormous pieces of furniture, curious

108 Henri Matisse
Interior with Etruscan Vase,
1940

111 Odilon Redon
The Eye, Like a Strange Balloon, 1882

154   Baudelaire's Voyages

Envole-toi bien loin de ces miasmes morbides;
Va te purifier dans l'air supérieur,
Et bois, comme une pure et divine liqueur,
Le feu clair qui remplit les espaces limpides.

From "Elévation"

Fly far away from these morbid miasmas;
purify yourself in the air above;
and drink, like a pure and divine liquor,
the clear fire that fills limpid space.

From "Elevation"

Dream-inspired images of interior spaces that provide comfort and even elation appear frequently in Baudelaire's poetry, but they are always, in the spirit of the poet's nature, countered and finally superseded by images of spaces that oppress. In "La Chambre double" ("The Double Room") Baudelaire at first finds himself in a room "qui ressemble à une rêverie, une chambre véritable *spirituelle*" ("that resembles a dream, a room truly *spiritual*"). It contains many of the same luxuries of the interior of "L'Invitation au voyage": furnishings that themselves have a dreamlike quality, fabrics that speak a muted language, flowers that he compares to sunsets, and a perfect lover, "la souveraine des rêves" ("the sovereign queen of dreams").[43] But then, just as he is convinced that this dream has erased time and eternity reigns, a knock at the door transforms dream into nightmare: "La chambre paradisiaque, l'idole, la souveraine des rêves . . . toute cette magie a disparu au coup brutal frappé par le Spectre" ("The chamber of paradise, the idol, the sovereign queen of dreams . . . all this magic has disappeared at the Specter's brutal knock"). It instantly becomes "ce taudis, ce séjour de l'éternel ennui" ("this hovel, this abode of eternel ennui"), which, he quickly remembers, is his real dwelling. In "La Cloche fêlée" ("The Cracked Bell"), he sits in his cold attic trying to warm himself before his fire and notes that his soul is not clear like the bell he hears chiming vigorously in the distance. His soul is cracked and can no longer fill the cold night with song. All he can do is sit in his constricted quarters and listen for "les souvenirs lointains lentement s'élever / Au bruit des carillons qui chantent dans la brume" ("distant

112 Edouard Manet
The Balloon, 1862

memories slowly to rise with the sound of the chimes that sing through the fog").

One of those devoutly wished-for memories might have contained the image of a Vermeer, with its soothing and restorative harmonies and intimations of the ideal. Another might well have been of the interior of that coach from years before, when he was a child nestled close to his mother, watching the sunset and thinking "traveling all the time would be a marvelous life for me" — as he donned his silk bonnet and began to dream.

113 Claude Monet
*Waterloo Bridge:
The Sun in a Fog,* 1903

Coda: *Voyage into the New*

Baudelaire was concerned about the future: both the place his poetry would hold and the voyages human beings would take in search of remedies for the human condition. In "Je te donne" he reveals his desire that his work inspire future poets and artists:

> Je te donne ces vers afin que si mon nom
> Aborde heureusement aux époques lointaines,

Et fait rêver un soir les cervelles humaines,
Vaisseau favorisé par un grand aquilon.

I give you these verses in case my name lands happily in some far-off time, inspires a dream, one evening, in a human mind; a vessel favored by the great north wind.

In "Le Voyage" he is more concerned with departures than arrivals. In the first section of the poem he writes:

Mais les vrais voyageurs sont ceux-là seuls qui
   partent
Pour partir; cœurs légers, semblables aux ballons,
De leur fatalité jamais ils ne s'écartent,
Et, sans savoir pourquoi, disent toujours: Allons!

But the true voyagers are only those who depart
for the sake of departure; hearts light as balloons,
they never refuse their fate and, without knowing
why, always say, Let's go!

In the last section of this poem, which he
intended to be the conclusion of *Les Fleurs du
mal,* in despair over all he has discovered on earlier voyages, he proposes a final journey:

O Mort, vieux capitaine, il est temps! levons
   l'ancre!
Ce pays nous ennuie, ô Mort! Appareillons!
Si le ciel et la mer sont noirs comme de l'encre,
Nos cœurs que tu connais sont remplis de rayons!

Verse-nous ton poison pour qu'il nous réconforte!
Nous voulons, tant ce feu nous brûle le cerveau,
Plonger au fond du gouffre, Enfer ou Ciel,
   qu'importe?

Au fond de l'inconnu pour trouver du *nouveau!*

O Death, old captain, it is time! raise the anchor!
This country makes us despair, O Death! let us
depart! If the sky and the sea are black as ink, our
hearts, as you know, are filled with light!

Pour us your poison, for it will comfort us! Do we
want, so much does this fire burn in our brains, to
plunge to the bottom of the abyss, Hell or Heaven,
it does not matter? On to the depths of the
Unknown to find something *new!*

Thus, at the conclusion of *Les Fleurs du mal*
Baudelaire offers an invitation to a voyage into the
new. Although he did not hold out much hope for
ultimate change, his invitation was enthusiastically accepted by artists of the twentieth century.
The essay by Dore Ashton that begins this book
traces the path of some of them as they filled in
the shapes of modernism that Baudelaire did so
much to outline. Here is the poet's meditation on
yet another journey, one taken in the company of
his dearest companion:

RECUEILLEMENT

Sois sage, ô ma Douleur, et tiens-toi plus tranquille.
Tu réclamais le Soir; il descend; le voici:
Une atmosphère obscure enveloppe la ville,
Aux uns portant la paix, aux autres le souci.

Pendant que des mortels la multitude vile,
Sous le fouet du Plaisir, ce bourreau sans merci,
Va cueillir des remords dans la fête servile,
Ma Douleur, donne-moi la main; viens par ici,

Loin d'eux. Vois se pencher les défuntes Années,
Sur les balcons du ciel, en robes surannées;
Surgir du fond des eaux le Regret souriant;

Le Soleil moribond s'endormir sous une arche,
Et, comme un long linceul traînant à l'Orient,
Entends, ma chère, entends la douce Nuit qui
   marche.

MEDITATION

Be wise, o my Sorrow, and be more tranquil.
You called for the evening; it comes; it is here:
an indistinct atmosphere envelops the city,
bringing peace to some, worry to others.

While those of the vile multitude,
under the whip of pleasure, that merciless torturer,
go to gather remorse in their servile revels,
give me your hand, my Sorrow; come this way,

Far from them. See the dead years lean down
from the balconies of the sky in their old gowns;
see smiling Regret loom up from the water's depths;

The dying sun is falling asleep under an arch,
and, like a long shroud trailing from the Orient,
listen, my dear one, listen as gentle Night approaches.

Notes   For an explanation of the citations to Baudelaire's works, see Preface and Acknowledgments, page 10.

Baudelaire, Irremediable Modern

1. Mayne, *Painter*, 13.
2. *Intimate Journals*, ed. and trans. Christopher Isherwood; Introduction by W. H. Auden (Hollywood: 1947), 96.
3. "Salon of 1859," Mayne, *Art*, 159.
4. On Delacroix's color see "The Exposition Universelle" in Mayne, *Art*, 141.
5. Fred Licht, *Goya: The Origins of the Modern Temper in Art* (New York: Universe, 1979), 89, 213.
6. T. S. Eliot, *Selected Essays* (London: Faber and Faber, 1930), 275, 377.
7. Cited in Grace Schulman, *Marianne Moore: The Poetry of Engagement* (Urbana and Chicago: University of Illinois Press, 1986), 28.
8. "The Life and Work of Eugène Delacroix," Mayne, *Painter*, 45.
9. "Salon of 1859," Mayne, *Art*, 159.
10. "Salon of 1846," ibid., 49.
11. Ibid., 50.
12. "Delacroix," Mayne, *Painter*, 52.
13. Henri Matisse, "Notes of a Painter" (1908), in Alfred H. Barr, Jr., *Matisse: His Art and his Public* (New York: Museum of Modern Art, 1951), 122, 119, 121.
14. *Picasso on Art*, ed. Dore Ashton (New York: Viking, 1972), 45.
15. *Conversations avec Cézanne*, ed. P. M. Doran (Paris, 1978), 13.
16. *Rodin on Art*, trans. from Paul Gsell by Mrs. Romilly Fedden (New York: Horizon, 1971), 44.
17. *Cézanne: Letters*, ed. John Rewald (1941; 4th ed., New York: Hacker Art Books, 1976), 324.
18. "Delacroix," Mayne, *Painter*, 47.
19. Ibid., 48.
20. "L'Art philosophique," Mayne, *Painter*, 204.
21. Théophile Gautier, "Notice" [1868], in *Edition définitive: Œuvres complètes de Charles Baudelaire* (Paris, 1868).
22. "Salon de 1846," Mayne, *Art*, 54.
23. Ibid., 97.
24. "Delacroix," Mayne, *Painter*, 58.
25. Octavio Paz, *Alternating Current* (New York: Viking, 1972), 32.
26. "The Exposition Universelle," Mayne, *Art*, 121–122.

27. André Breton, *Surrealism and Painting*, trans. Simon W. Taylor (New York: Harper and Row, 1972), 197. The Baudelaire quotation is from "Delacroix."
28. Ibid.
29. Dore Ashton, *The New York School: A Cultural Reckoning* (New York: Viking, 1972), 61.
30. "Richard Wagner and Tannhäuser in Paris," Mayne, *Painter*, 116, 117, 143.
31. Statement in *Twentieth-Century Artists on Art*, Dore Ashton, ed. (New York: Pantheon, 1985), 119.

Beacons

1. *The Letters of Gustave Flaubert 1857–1880*, ed. and trans. Francis Steegmuller (Cambridge, MA: Harvard University Press, 1957), 20. The letters noted here and in note 2 are dated 1860, three years after both *Madame Bovary* and *Les Fleurs du mal* were brought before the French court on charges of obscenity. Flaubert was acquitted and Baudelaire convicted. In spite of this critique of the poet by the novelist, the two writers admired and supported each other.
2. *Selected Letters of Charles Baudelaire: The Conquest of Solitude*, ed. and trans. Rosemary Lloyd (Chicago: University of Chicago Press, 1986), 155.
3. The generic title for Baudelaire's volume of prose poems is *Petits Poèmes en prose (Little Poems in Prose)* and has been used for several editions. Baudelaire proposed *Le Rôdeur Parisien (The Parisian Prowler)* in a letter to one of his editors. *Le Spleen de Paris (Paris Spleen)* is the title in Pichois's *Œuvres complètes* and is used throughout this book. For a more detailed discussion see Charles Baudelaire, *The Parisian Prowler*, ed. Edward K. Kaplan (Athens: University of Georgia Press, 1989), xi–xii.
4. Martin Turnell, *Baudelaire: A Study of His Poetry* (New York: New Directions, 1972), 160.
5. Mayne, *Art*, 156.
6. Charles Baudelaire, *Correspondance*, ed. Claude Pichois (Paris: Gallimard, Bibliothèque de la Pléiade, 1973), 1:458.
7. Lloyd, 148.
8. Mayne, *Art*, 159.
9. Lloyd, 16.

10. Georges Poulet and Robert Kopp, *Baudelaire: The Artist and His World*, trans. Robert Allen and James Emmons (Geneva: Editions d'Art Albert Skira, 1969), 30.
11. Mayne, *Art*, 166.
12. The edition of *Les Fleurs du mal* illustrated with works of visual art that may have inspired Baudelaire, edited by Jean Pommier and Claude Pichois (Paris: Club des Librairies de France, 1959; reprint Paris: Editions A. Balland, 1967), is one of the most valuable sources of information on this subject. See PAGE 487 for the editors' comments on inspiration for "La Béatrice."
13. Mayne, *Art*, 139.
14. Ibid.
15. Mayne, *Painter*, 190.
16. Mayne, *Art*, 44.
17. Ibid., 56–57.
18. Jean Prévost, *Baudelaire: Essai sur la création et l'inspiration poétiques* (Paris: Mercure de France, 1971, written 1943–44), 116.
19. Quoted in Marcel Raymond, *From Baudelaire to Surrealism* (New York: Wittenborn, Schultz, 1949), 18.
20. Quoted in Alison Fairlie, "Aspects of Expression in Baudelaire's Art Criticism," in *French Nineteenth Century Painting and Literature*, ed. Ulrich Finke (New York: Harper and Row, 1972), 42.

Voyage into the Depths

1. *Selected Letters of Charles Baudelaire: The Conquest of Solitude*, ed. and trans. Rosemary Lloyd (Chicago: University of Chicago Press, 1986), 8.
2. Charles Baudelaire, *Correspondance*, ed. Claude Pichois (Paris: Gallimard, Bibliothèque de la Pléiade, 1973), 1:303.
3. Comparisons of Baudelaire and Dostoyevski are made in John Middleton Murry, "Baudelaire," in *Baudelaire: A Collection of Critical Essays*, ed. Henri Peyre (Englewood Cliffs, NJ: Prentice Hall, 1962), and Joseph D. Bennet, *Baudelaire: A Criticism* (Princeton: Princeton University Press, 1946).
4. Mayne, *Painter*, 192.

39. Paul Valéry, "The Triumph of Manet," in *Manet: A Retrospective*, 293.

40. George Mauner, *Manet Peintre Philosophe: A Study of the Painter's Themes* (University Park: Pennsylvania State University Press, 1975), 159. The idea of the absinthe drinker as a *homo-duplex*, a man leading a double life, is developed here.

41. See Larry Ligo, "Manet's *Le Vieux Musicien*, an Artistic Manifesto Acknowledging the Influences of Baudelaire and Photography upon His Work," *Gazette des Beaux-Arts* 110 (December 1987): 233, 237 NOTES 9–10.

42. Mayne, *Art*, 118.

43. Quoted in Theodore Reff, *Manet and Modern Paris* (Washington, D.C.: National Gallery of Art, 1983), 173. See Reff here for development of Manet's interest in the impoverished areas of Paris.

44. Burton, 67.

45. Mauner, 52–53.

46. Quoted in Francis Haskell, "The Sad Clown: Some Notes on a Nineteenth Century Myth," *French Nineteenth Century Painting and Literature*, ed. Ulrich Fink (New York: Harper and Row, 1972), 9.

47. Paula Hays Harper, *Daumier's Clowns: Les Saltimbanques et les Parades* (New York: Garland Press, 1981), 2.

48. Wallace Fowlie, *Poem and Symbol: A Brief History of French Symbolism* (University Park: Pennsylvania State University Press, 1990), 55.

49. Harper, 79.

50. Theodore Reff, "Saltimbanques, Clowns and Fools," *Artforum* (October 1971): 38.

51. *Don Juan* IV:4, quoted in Haskell, 14.

52. Baudelaire took notice of Daumier's plight in a letter to his friend and publisher Auguste Poulet-Malassis, writing, "Think about Daumier! about Daumier, unemployed, booted out the door of *Charivari*" (*Correspondance*, 2:9).

53. Harper, 100.

54. Henry James, *Daumier, Caricaturist* (London: Rodale, 1954), 36.

55. Guillaume Apollinaire, *Apollinaire on Art: Essays and Reviews 1902–1918*, ed. Leroy C. Breunig, trans. Susan Suleiman (New York: Viking, 1972; reprint New York: Da Capo, n.d.), 16.

56. Reff, "Saltimbanques," 32.

57. Pierre Courthion, *Rouault* (New York: Harry N. Abrams, 1977), 104.

58. William A. Dyrness, *Rouault: A Vision of Suffering and Salvation* (Grand Rapids, MI: William B. Eerdmans, 1971), 149.

59. Mona Hadler, "William Baziotes, A Contemporary Poet-Painter," *Arts Magazine* 51 (June 1977): 106–107.

60. Ibid., 105.

61. Quoted in Juliet Wilson-Bareau, *Manet by himself* (Boston: Bulfinch Press, Little, Brown, 1991), 44.

62. Hemmings, 215.

63. Perruchot, 149.

64. Quoted in Wilson-Bareau, 44.

65. The volume, *Charles Baudelaire, sa vie et son œuvre* (Paris: Alphonse Le Merre, 1869), contains two etched portraits of Baudelaire by Manet as well as several etched portraits (two of Baudelaire and one of Courbet) by Félix Bracquemond.

66. Although not all scholars agree that this painting portrays Baudelaire's funeral, Theodore Reff makes a convincing case for it. See Reff, *Manet and Modern Paris*, 40–41.

Voyage into the Dream

1. Baudelaire knew Whistler, praised his *Thames Etchings*, and, not long before *Harmony in Blue and Silver: Trouville* was painted, put his name on a list of people to whom his books should be sent. Whistler's starting point for this portrait of the artist contemplating the sea was probably Gustave Courbet's *The Seashore at Palavas* (1854), a very similar composition. However, whereas the figure in Courbet's painting enthusiastically salutes the realistic panorama before him, Whistler's figure pensively contemplates a dreamlike seascape, as does Baudelaire in his meditation on the condition of the artist in "Le Confiteor de l'artiste" (most likely written at Honfleur on the Normandy coast, very near Trouville, in 1859). Whistler's rejection of Courbet's realism during this period in favor of an art based on the temperament of the artist corresponds exactly to Baudelaire's earlier break with Courbet and the poet-critic's statement in his "Salon de 1859" that "the true artist" and "the true poet should only paint in accordance with what he sees and feels." He must not be faithful to reality like the pedant but "*really* faithful to his own nature" (Mayne, *Art*, 155) — just as this painting corresponds to his poem.

2. Jean-Paul Sartre, *Baudelaire*, trans. Martin Turnell (New York: New Directions, 1950), 53.

3. *Selected Letters of Charles Baudelaire: The Conquest of Solitude*, ed. and trans. Rosemary Lloyd (Chicago: University of Chicago Press, 1986), 3.

4. Mayne, *Painter*, 47–48.

5. In "The Painter of Modern Life" Baudelaire devotes a chapter to the virtues of *maquillage*, the use of facial makeup. He writes, "Good is always the product of some art," and asks his readers "to scrutinize whatever is natural." "You will find," he tells them, "nothing but frightfulness. Everything beautiful and noble is the result of reason and calculation" (Mayne, *Painter*, 32). In everyday life *maquillage* is an extension of these notions. "Anyone," he claims, "can see that the use of rice-powder, so stupidly anathematized by our Arcadian philosophers, is successfully designed to rid the complexion of those blemishes that Nature has outrageously strewn there, and thus to create an abstract unity in the color and texture of the skin, a unity which like that produced by the tights of a dancer, immediately approximates the human being to the statue, that is to something superior and divine" (ibid., 33). Baudelaire himself was a sometime user of facial makeup. Manet, who often teased him about this habit, said to Antonin Proust, "he really lays it on, but there is so much genius beneath the layer" (Antonin Proust, "Edouard Manet: Souvenirs," in *Manet: A Retrospective*, ed. T. A. Gronberg; New York: Park Lane, 1988, 50).

6. Pere Gimferrer, *Giorgio de Chirico* (New York: Rizzoli, 1988), 15.

7. Giorgio de Chirico, *Memoirs of Giorgio de Chirico*, trans. Margaret Crosland (London: Peter Owen, 1971), 220.

8. According to F. W. Leakey, "Rêve parisien" may have been inspired by a work of visual art. He writes, "In two prose texts of 1859, Baudelaire alludes to a drawing by an English architect which dazzled and astounded him at the Paris Universal Exhibition of 1855. . . . This water-color drawing can be identified as the *Architectural Composition* by H. E. Kendall, Jr. . . . and may perhaps have been further remembered by Baudelaire in the imagery of his poem 'Rêve parisien.'" See Leakey, *Baudelaire: Collected Essays, 1953–1988*, ed. Eva Jacobs (Cambridge: Cambridge University Press, 1990), 227. (The drawing is illustrated there as PLATE 14.) Pommier and Pichois in their edition of *Les Fleurs du mal* (Paris: Club des Librairies de France, 1959; reprint Paris: Editions A. Balland, 1967), 483, 485, discuss Leakey's idea and propose that Piranesi's architectural drawings with their ominous qualities are more in tune with the "*terrible*" aspect of Baudelaire's poem and may have inspired "Rêve parisien."

9. Lloyd, 151.

10. Christophe's sculpture, *La Comédie humaine*, was located in the Tuileries Gardens from the time of its installation there in 1876 until recently when it was moved to the Musée d'Orsay. See FIG. 26.

11. Prévost, *Baudelaire: Essai sur la création et l'inspiration poétiques* (Paris: Mercure de France, 1971), 27.

12. Paul Gauguin, *Paul Gauguin's Intimate Journals,* trans. Van Wyck Brooks (New York: Liveright, 1921), 41.

13. Paul Gauguin, *Noa Noa,* trans. O. F. Theis, reprinted in *Gauguin: A Retrospective,* Marla Prather and Charles F. Stuckey, eds. (New York: Park Lane, 1987), 170.

14. Louis Aragon, *Matisse: A Novel,* trans. Jean Stewart, 2 vols. (New York: Harcourt Brace Jovanovich and Helen and Kurt Wolff, 1971), 2:11.

15. Ibid., 2:21, 23.

16. See Pierre Schneider, *Matisse* (Paris: Flammarion, 1984), 738.

17. Jack D. Flam, *Matisse on Art* (New York: E. P. Dutton, 1973), 49.

18. Schneider, 738.

19. See John Elderfield, *The Cut-outs of Henri Matisse* (New York: George Braziller, 1978), 32.

20. Schneider, 698.

21. Isabelle Monod-Fontaine et al., *Œuvres de Henri Matisse* (Paris: Editions du Centre Pompidou, 1989), 381–382, N. 1 (my trans.).

22. Schneider, 698.

23. Monod-Fontaine, 382 (my trans.).

24. Matisse wrote to Claude Camoin that he had completed the illustrations for *Les Fleurs du mal:* "I've done thirty-five lithographs of expressive heads to match the pieces chosen. It is not what is usually expected of illustrations for this poet. It would be easy to imagine a series of legs writhing in the air in some degree of agony. I hope that the middle classes will not be so demanding and that they will make allowances for the unexpected in my work" (quoted in Margrit Hahnloser, *Matisse: The Graphic Work,* New York: Rizzoli, 1988, 182).

25. Mayne, *Art,* 47.

26. See Richard D. E. Burton, *Baudelaire in 1859: A Study in the Sources of Poetic Creativity* (Cambridge: Cambridge University Press, 1988), 12, and Pichois, *Œuvres complètes,* 1:1345, for discussions of Baudelaire's view from the belvedere.

27. Mayne, *Art,* 199–200.

28. Ibid., 200.

29. Pichois, *Œuvres complètes,* 2:1311.

30. Henry Vidal, "Remembering Claude Monet," reprinted in *Monet: A Retrospective,* Charles F. Stuckey, ed. (New York: Park Lane, 1985), 349.

31. Mayne, *Art,* 220.

32. See Lois Boe Hyslop, *Baudelaire: Man of His Time* (New Haven: Yale University Press, 1980), 9; and Frances Suzman Jowell, *Thoré-Bürger and the Art of the Past* (New York: Garland, 1977), 243–260.

33. Lloyd, 96.

34. Burton, 10. For a complete and extraordinarily fine analysis of the effect of Baudelaire's stay in Honfleur on his creative output, see Burton's chapter "Baudelaire at Honfleur," 1–63.

35. Baudelaire, *Correspondance,* ed. Claude Pichois (Paris: Gallimard, Bibliothèque de la Pléiade, 1973), 2:626.

36. Lloyd, 148.

37. See FIG. 105 and NOTE 26, above.

38. John Michael Montias, *Vermeer and His Milieu* (Princeton: Princeton University Press, 1989), 197–199.

39. Zbigniew Herbert, *Still Life with a Bridle,* trans. John and Bogdana Carpenter (New York: Ecco Press, 1991), 105–106.

40. Peter C. Sutton, *Masters of Seventeenth Century Dutch Genre Painting* (Philadelphia: Philadelphia Museum of Art, 1984), 361.

41. For the most complete consideration of Baudelaire's inspiration by Dutch interiors in "L'Invitation au voyage," see Jean-Bertrand Barrère, "Chemins, échoes et images dans 'L'Invitation au voyage' de Baudelaire," *Revue de littérature comparée* 31.4 (December 1957): 483–484 (quoted passage, my trans.).

42. Brooks Adams, "The Poetics of Odilon Redon's 'Closed Eyes,'" *Arts Magazine* 54.5 (January 1980): 12.

43. It should be noted that in "La Chambre double" Baudelaire's description of the perfect space is idealized to the point that he even banishes all representational art from the walls, which he calls blasphemous in relation to the "rêve pur" ("pure dream").

Selected Bibliography

William Baziotes (1912–1963)

Hadler, Mona. "William Baziotes, A Contemporary Poet-Painter." *Arts Magazine* 51 (June 1977): 102–110.

Polcari, Stephen. *Abstract Expressionism and the Modern Experience.* Cambridge: Cambridge University Press, 1991.

Eugène Boudin (1824–1898)

Benjamin, Ruth L. *Eugène Boudin.* New York: Raymond and Raymond, 1937.

Jean-Aubry, G., with Robert Schmit. *Eugène Boudin.* Translated by Caroline Tisdall. Greenwich, CT: New York Graphic Society, 1968.

Selz, Jean. *Boudin.* Translated by Shirley Jennings. New York: Crown Publishers, 1982.

Félix Buhot (1847–1898)

Fisher, Jay McKean, and Colles Baxter. *Félix Buhot, Peintre-Graveur: Prints, Drawings, and Paintings.* Baltimore, MD: Baltimore Museum of Art, 1983.

Paul Cézanne (1839–1906)

Ashton, Dore. *A Fable of Modern Art.* London: Thames and Hudson, 1980.

Bernard, Emile. *Souvenirs sur Paul Cézanne, une conversation avec Cézanne.* Paris: Michel, 1926.

Lewis, Mary Tompkins. *Cézanne's Early Imagery.* Berkeley: University of California Press, 1989.

Lindsay, Jack. *Cézanne: His Life and Art.* Greenwich, CT: New York Graphic Society, 1969.

Rilke, Rainer Maria. *Letters on Cézanne.* Edited by Clara Rilke. Translated by Joel Agee. New York: Fromm International Publishing Corporation, 1985.

Gustave Courbet (1819–1877)

Bowness, Alan. "Courbet and Baudelaire." *Gazette des Beaux-Arts* (December 1977): **194**.

Fried, Michael. *Courbet's Realism.* Chicago: University of Chicago Press, 1990.

Gustave Courbet 1819–1877. Philadelphia Museum of Art and Museum of Fine Arts, Boston. 1959.

Lindsay, Jack. *Gustave Courbet: His Life and Art.* London: Jupiter, 1977.

Honoré Daumier (1808–1879)

Adhémar, Jean. *Honoré Daumier.* Paris, 1954.

Drost, Wolfgang. "L'Inspiration plastique chez Baudelaire." *Gazette des Beaux-Arts* (May–June 1957): 321–336.

Harper, Paula Hays. *Daumier's Clowns: Les Saltimbanques et les Parades.* New York: Garland Press, 1981.

Starobinski, Jean. *Portrait de l'artiste en saltimbanque.* Geneva, 1970.

Symmons, Sarah. *Daumier.* London: Oresko Books, 1979.

Vincent, Howard P. *Daumier and His World.* Evanston, IL: Northwestern University Press, 1968.

Eugène Delacroix (1798–1863)

Abel, Elizabeth. "Redefining the Sister Arts: Baudelaire's Response to the Art of Delacroix." *Critical Inquiry* 6 (Spring 1980): 363–384.

Moss, Armand. *Baudelaire et Delacroix.* Paris: A. G. Nizet, 1973.

Prévost, Jean. *Baudelaire: Essai sur la création et l'inspiration poétiques.* Paris: Mercure de France, 1971.

Albrecht Dürer (1471–1528)

Dodwell, R. "Dürer's Melancholia in Nineteenth-century French and English Art and Literature." *Zeitschrift des deutschen Vereins für Kunstwissenschaft* 30.1–4 (1976): **67–85**.

Patty, James S. "Baudelaire and Dürer: Avatars of Melancholia." *Symposium* 38.3 (Fall 1984): 244–257.

Edouard Manet (1832–1883)

Collins, Bradford R. "Manet's *Luncheon in the Studio:* An Homage to Baudelaire." *Art Journal* 38.2 (Winter 1978/79): **107–113**.

Fried, Michael. "Painting Memories: On the Containment of the Past in Baudelaire and Manet." *Critical Inquiry* 10.3 (March 1984): 510–542.

Hamilton, George Heard. *Manet and His Critics.* New York: W. W. Norton, 1969.

Hanson, Anne Coffin. *Edouard Manet 1832–1883.* Philadelphia and Chicago: Philadelphia Museum of Art and The Art Institute of Chicago, 1966.

_____. *Manet and the Modern Tradition.* New Haven: Yale University Press, 1977.

_____. "Popular Imagery and the Work of Edouard Manet." In *French Nineteenth Century Painting and Literature,* edited by Ulrich Finke. New York: Harper and Row, 1972, **133–163**.

Hyslop, Lois Boe, and Francis E. Hyslop. "Baudelaire and Manet: A Re-appraisal." In *Baudelaire as a Love Poet and Other Essays,* edited by Lois Boe Hyslop. University Park: Pennsylvania State University Press, 1969, **87–130**.

Leiris, Alain de. "Baudelaire's Assessment of Manet." In Ellen Eisenberg, *Hommage à Baudelaire.* University of Maryland Art Gallery (1968), 5–10.

_____. *The Drawings of Edouard Manet.* Berkeley and Los Angeles: University of California Press, 1969.

Ligo, Larry. "The Luncheon in the Studio: Manet's Reaffirmation of the Influences of Baudelaire and Photography upon His Work." *Arts Magazine* 61.5 (January 1987): 46–51.

_____. "Manet's Frontispiece Etchings: His Symbolic Self-Portrait Acknowledging the Influences of Baudelaire and Photography upon His Work." *Gazette des Beaux-Arts* 108 (September 1986): 66–74.

_____. "Manet's *Le Vieux Musicien,* an Artistic Manifesto Acknowledging the Influences of Baudelaire and Photography upon His Work." *Gazette des Beaux-Arts* 110 (December 1987): 232–238.

Manet by himself, edited by Juliet Wilson-Bareau. Boston: Bulfinch Press/Little, Brown and Co., 1991.

Mauner, George. "Baudelaire, Manet and the Recurrent Theme." *Yearbook of Comparative Criticism* 1 (1968): **244–257**.

_____. *Manet Peintre Philosophe: A Study of the Painter's Themes.* University Park: Pennsylvania State University Press, 1975.

Proust, Antonin. *Edouard Manet: Souvenirs.* Paris: H. Laurens, 1913.

Reff, Theodore. *Manet and Modern Paris.* Washington, DC: National Gallery of Art, 1983.

Reybeyrol, Philippe. "Baudelaire et Manet." *Les Temps Modernes* (October 1949): 705–725.

Shiff, Richard. "Remembering Impressions." *Critical Inquiry* 12.2 (Winter 1986): **439–448**.

Tabarant, Adolphe. *Manet et ses œuvres.* Paris: Gallimard, 1947.

Valéry, Paul. "The Triumph of Manet." In *Manet: A Retrospective,* edited by T. A. Gronberg. New York: Park Lane, 1988.

Zola, Emile. "Edouard Manet." In *Manet: A Retrospective,* edited by T. A. Gronberg. New York: Park Lane, 1988.

Henri Matisse (1869–1954)

Aragon, Louis. *Henri Matisse: A Novel.* Translated by Jean Stewart. 2 vols. New York: Harcourt Brace Jovanovich and Helen and Kurt Wolff, 1971.

Benjamin, Roger. *Matisse's "Notes of a Painter."* Ann Arbor: UMI Research Press, 1987.

Eichorn, Linda. "Matisse and *Les Fleurs du mal.*" *The Library Chronicle of the University of Texas at Austin* 27 (1984): 46–59.

Flam, Jack D. *Matisse, The Man and His Art. 1869–1918.* Ithaca and London: Cornell University Press, 1986.

———. *Matisse on Art.* New York: E. P. Dutton, 1978.

Hahnloser, Margrit. *Matisse: The Graphic Work.* New York: Rizzoli, 1988.

Monod-Fontaine, Isabelle, et al. *Œuvres de Henri Matisse.* Paris: Editions du Centre Pompidou, 1989.

Schneider, Pierre. *Matisse.* Paris: Flammarion, 1984.

Charles Méryon (1821–1868)

Burke, James D. *Charles Méryon: Prints and Drawings.* Toledo Museum of Art, Yale University Art Gallery, St. Louis Art Museum, 1974.

Hyslop, Lois Boe, and Francis E. Hyslop. "Baudelaire and Méryon: Painters of the Urban Landscape." *Symposium* 38.3 (Fall 1984): 196–220.

Edvard Munch (1863–1944)

Munch et la France. Paris: Musée d'Orsay, 1991.

Stang, Ragna. *Edvard Munch.* Translated by Geoffrey Culverwell. New York: Abbeville Press, 1979.

Timm, Werner. *The Graphic Art of Edvard Munch.* Translated by Ruth Michaelis-Jena and Patrick Murray. Greenwich, CT: New York Graphic Society, 1972.

Torjusen, Bente. *Words and Images of Edvard Munch.* Chelsea, VT: Chelsea Green Publishing, 1986.

Odilon Redon (1840–1916)

Adams, Brooks. "The Poetics of Odilon Redon's 'Closed Eyes.'" *Arts Magazine* 54.5 (January 1980): 12–13 ff.

Hyslop, Lois Boe, and Francis E. Hyslop. "Redon's Debt to the Critical Essays of Baudelaire." *Nineteenth Century French Studies* 15.1–2 (1986): 141–161.

Rewald, John, Harold Joachim, and Dore Ashton. *Odilon Redon, Gustave Moreau, Rodolphe Bresdin.* Museum of Modern Art and Art Institute of Chicago. Garden City, NY: Doubleday, 1961.

Seznec, Jean. "Odilon Redon and Literature." In *French Nineteenth Century Painting and Literature.* Edited by Ulrich Finke. New York: Harper and Row, 1972, 280–298.

Strieter, Terry W. "Odilon Redon and Charles Baudelaire: Some Parallels." *Art Journal* 35.1 (Fall 1975): 17–19.

Auguste Rodin (1840–1917)

Baudelaire, Charles. *Vingt-sept Poèmes de Fleurs du mal.* Preface by Camille Mauclair. Illustrations by Auguste Rodin. Paris: La Société des "Amis du Livre Moderne," 1918.

Elsen, Albert E. *The Gates of Hell by Auguste Rodin.* Stanford, CA: Stanford University Press, 1985.

———. *Rodin.* New York: Museum of Modern Art, 1963.

Judrin, Claude. *Rodin et les écrivains de son temps; sculpteurs, dessins, lettres et livres du fonds Rodin.* Paris: Musée Rodin, June 23–October 18, 1976.

Thorson, Victoria. *Rodin Graphics: A Catalogue Raisonné of Drypoints and Book Illustrations.* San Francisco: San Francisco Museum of Fine Arts, 1975.

Félicien Rops (1833–1898)

Arwas, Victor, and Philip Ward-Jackson. *Félicien Rops.* Arts Council of Great Britain, 1976–1977.

Les Fleurs du mal: Félicien Rops and Charles Baudelaire. Rijksmuseum Vincent van Gogh, June 12–September 2, 1985.

Hoffman, Edith. "Notes on the Iconography of Félicien Rops." *Burlington Magazine* 123.937 (April 1981): 206–218.

Holtzman, Ellen. "Félicien Rops and Baudelaire: Evolution of a Frontispiece." *Art Journal* 38.2 (Winter 1978–79), 102–106.

Legrand, Francine-Claire. "Rops et Baudelaire." *Gazettes des Beaux-Arts* 108 (September 1986): 191–200.

Georges Rouault (1871–1958)

Chapon, François. *Œuvre Gravé Rouault.* Catalogue Établi par Isabelle Rouault avec la collaboration d'Olivier Nouaille Rouault. 2 vols. Monte Carlo: André Sauret, 1978.

Courthion, Pierre. *Rouault.* New York: Harry N. Abrams, 1977.

Dyrness, William A. *Rouault: A Vision of Suffering and Salvation.* Grand Rapids, MI: William B. Eerdmans Publishing, 1971.

Guignard, Jacques. *The Fourteen Engravings [by Rouault] for "Les Fleurs du mal."* London: Eskanazi, June–July 1972.

List of Illustrations

Charles Baudelaire in Profile Wearing a Hat *(Charles Baudelaire de profil en chapeau),* 1862 **67**
Etching, 3¾ × 3¼"
Private Collection

The Gypsies *(Les gitanos),* 1862
Etching, 12½ × 9¼"
S. P. Avery Collection, The Miriam and Ira D. Wallach Division of Art, Prints and Photographs, The New York Public Library, Astor, Lenox and Tilden Foundations

The Little Girl *(La petite fille),* 1862
Etching and drypoint, 8⅛ × 4⅞"
S. P. Avery Collection, The Miriam and Ira D. Wallach Division of Art, Prints and Photographs, The New York Public Library, Astor, Lenox and Tilden Foundations

Lola de Valence, 1862
Etching, 10⅜ × 7¼"
S. P. Avery Collection, The Miriam and Ira D. Wallach Division of Art, Prints and Photographs, The New York Public Library, Astor, Lenox and Tilden Foundations

Olympia, 1865
Etching and aquatint, 3½ × 7"
S. P. Avery Collection, The Miriam and Ira D. Wallach Division of Art, Prints and Photographs, The New York Public Library, Astor, Lenox and Tilden Foundations

Cats' Rendezvous *(Le rendez-vous des chats),* 1868 **114**
Lithograph, 17½ × 13⅛"
S. P. Avery Collection, The Miriam and Ira D. Wallach Division of Art, Prints and Photographs, The New York Public Library, Astor, Lenox and Tilden Foundations

At the Window *(A la fenêtre),* 1875 **59**
Plate 3 from *Le Corbeau*
Transfer lithograph, 15⅛ × 11⅞"
S. P. Avery Collection, The Miriam and Ira D. Wallach Division of Art, Prints and Photographs, The New York Public Library, Astor, Lenox and Tilden Foundations

Under the Lamp *(Sous le lampe),* 1875
Plate 1 from *Le Corbeau*
Transfer lithograph, 10⅞ × 14¾"
S. P. Avery Collection, The Miriam and Ira D. Wallach Division of Art, Prints and Photographs, The New York Public Library, Astor, Lenox and Tilden Foundations

Henri Matisse (French, 1869–1954)

The Swan *(Le Cygne),* 1931 **79**
Illustration for "Plusieurs Sonnets," *Poésies de Stéphane Mallarmé*
Etching, 13¼ × 9¾"
The Brooklyn Museum, Carll H. de Silver Fund, 36.67.23

Portrait of Baudelaire, 1932 **49**
Illustration for "Le Tombeau de Charles Baudelaire," *Poésies de Stéphane Mallarmé*
Etching, 13¼ × 9¾"
The Brooklyn Museum, Carll H. de Silver Fund, 36.67.26

The Windows *(Les Fenêtres),* 1932
Illustration for "Soupir," *Poésies de Stéphane Mallarmé*
Etching, 13¼ × 9¾"
The Brooklyn Museum, Carll H. de Silver Fund, 36.67.5

Icarus, 1943
Plate VIII from *Jazz,* 1947
Color stencil, 16¼ × 10¾"
Richard Zeisler, New York

A Former Life *(La Vie antérieure),* 1944 **98**
Illustration for *Les Fleurs du mal,* 1947
Photolithograph, 11¼ × 9¹⁄₁₆"
Spencer Collection, The New York Public Library, Astor, Lenox and Tilden Foundations

The Fall of Icarus *(La Chute d'Icare),* 1945 **46**
Frontispiece, *Verve* magazine, #13, November 1945
Lithograph, 13¼ × 10³⁄₁₆"
Special Collections Department, University Libraries, State University of New York at Stony Brook

Martinique Woman *(Martiniquaise),* 1946–1947
Etching, 16 × 10¹⁵⁄₁₆"
Collection Grunwald Center for the Graphic Arts, UCLA. Gift of Mr. and Mrs. Stanley I. Talpis

Self-Portrait, Three-Quarter View, 1948 **99**
Lithograph, 9 × 7¼"
The Museum of Modern Art, New York. Curt Valentin Bequest

Sadness of the King *(Tristesse du Roi),* 1952
From *Verve* magazine, #27–28, 1952–1953
Lithograph, 14¾ × 20⅞"
Special Collections Department, University Libraries, State University of New York at Stony Brook

Michael Mazur (American, b. 1935)

Portrait of Baudelaire after Rodin, c. 1981
Monotype, 31¾ × 23⅞"
Gift of Michael Mazur and David R. Godine in memory of Morton Godine, Miriam and Ira D. Wallach Division of Art, Prints and Photographs, The New York Public Library, Astor, Lenox and Tilden Foundations

Charles Méryon (French, 1821–1868)

Le Stryge, 1853 **57**
Etching and drypoint, 6⅝ × 5¹⁄₁₆"
The Metropolitan Museum of Art, Bequest of Mrs. H. O. Havemeyer, 1929. The H. O. Havemeyer Collection

The Exchange Bridge *(Le Pont-au-Change),* 1854
Etching, 2nd state, 6⅛ × 13³⁄₁₆"
Courtesy of The Fogg Art Museum, Harvard University Art Museums, Bequest of Joseph B. Marvin

Turret, rue de l'Ecole-de-Médecin *(Tourelle, rue de l'Ecole-de-Médecin),* 1861
Etching and drypoint, 12th state, 8⁵⁄₁₆ × 5¹³⁄₁₆"
Private Collection

The Street of Cantors *(Rue des Chantres),* 1862 **62**
Etching and drypoint, 11¹³⁄₁₆ × 5¹³⁄₁₆"
Yale University Art Gallery. Gift of Allen Evarts Foster, B.A. 1906

Oceania, Fishing near Palm Trees *(Océanie, pêche aux palmes),* 1863
Etching, 4⁹⁄₁₆ × 11⁹⁄₁₆"
The Carnegie Museum of Art, Pittsburgh, Andrew Carnegie Fund, 17.30.18

Frans van Mieris (Dutch, 1635–1681)

Interior with Figures Playing Tric-Trac, 1680
Oil on canvas, 30½ × 26½"
Sarah Campbell Blaffer Foundation, Houston, Texas

Robert Motherwell (American, 1915–1991)

The Voyage Ten Years After, 1961 **5**
Oil on canvas, 69 × 210¼"
Collection Dedalus Foundation (at Heckscher Museum only)

Selections from the Lyric Suite, 1965
Colored ink on rice paper, 9 × 11" (each)
Collection Dedalus Foundation

Edvard Munch (Norwegian, 1863–1944)

Moonlight, 1895
Drypoint and aquatint, 12³⁄₁₆ × 10"
The Museum of Modern Art, New York, Abby Aldrich Rockefeller Fund

The Scream, 1895
Lithograph, 13⅞ × 9¹³⁄₁₆″
Epstein Family Collection

Vampire, 1895
Lithograph, 15⅛ × 21¾″
Epstein Family Collection

Anxiety, 1896   **71**
Lithograph, printed in two colors, 16¼ × 15¼″
Epstein Family Collection

The Urn, 1896   **34**
Lithograph, 18³⁄₁₆ × 10½″
Epstein Family Collection

Charles Neyt (Belgian; dates unknown)
Portrait of Charles Baudelaire, 1864–1865
Photogravure of photograph in *Charles Baude-
laire Œuvres posthumes* (Paris, 1887), 4⅜ × 2⅞″
Private Collection

Pablo Picasso (Spanish, 1881–1973)
Saltimbanque Resting (*Le saltimbanque au
repos*), 1905
Drypoint, 4¾ × 3⁷⁄₁₆″
The Museum of Modern Art, New York. Gift of
Abby Aldrich Rockefeller

Giovanni Piranesi (Italian, 1720–1778)
The Staircase with Trophies, 1761   **21**
Plate 8 from *Carceri,* 2nd edition
Etching, 21⅞ × 16″
Print Collection, The Miriam and Ira D. Wallach
Division of Art, Prints and Photographs, The
New York Public Library, Astor, Lenox and Til-
den Foundations

Jackson Pollock (American, 1912–1956)
Untitled, 1944–1945
Engraving and drypoint on ivory wove paper,
19³⁄₁₆ × 27¼″
Pollock-Krasner House and Study Center

Untitled, 1944–1945
Engraving and drypoint on ivory wove paper,
20 × 13⅝″
Pollock-Krasner House and Study Center

Odilon Redon (French, 1840–1916)
Closed Eyes (*Les yeux clos*), c. 1890   **109**
Oil on canvas, 25¾ × 20″
Smith College Museum of Art, Northampton,
Massachusetts. Gift of Mrs. Charles Inslee
(Marguerite Tuthill Inslee '15), 1956 (at Heck-
scher Museum only)

Ceaselessly the Devil Stirs at My Side (*Sans
cesse à mes côtés s'agite le démon*), 1890   **25**
Etching, 8½ × 7″
The Howard L. and Muriel Weingrow Collec-
tion of Avant-Garde Art and Literature, Axinn
Library, Hofstra University, Hempstead, New
York

Auguste Rodin (French, 1840–1917)
I Am Beautiful (*Je suis belle*), 1882   **40**
Bronze, 27¾ × 12 × 12½″
Rodin Museum, Philadelphia. Gift of Jules E.
Mastbaum

L'Irréparable, c. 1887–1888
Illustration in *Les Fleurs du mal,* Paris: The Lim-
ited Editions Club, 1940. Preface by Camille
Mauclair
Collotype of a drawing in pen and ink, ink
wash, and white gouache on paper, page size:
8⅞ × 6⅞″
Private Collection

Head of Baudelaire, 1898
Bronze, 8⅞ × 7¾ × 9″, cast c. 1954–1960
Hirshhorn Museum and Sculpture Garden,
Smithsonian Institution. Gift of Joseph H.
Hirshhorn, 1966

Félicien Rops (Belgian, 1833–1898)
Satan Sowing Tares (*Satan semant l'ivraie*),
undated
Aquatint and soft-ground etching, 14³⁄₁₆ × 10⅜″
National Gallery of Art, Washington, DC,
Rosenwald Collection 1951.10.401

Frontispiece: The Waifs (*Les Epaves*), 1868   **36**
Etching, 6⁵⁄₁₆ × 4″
National Gallery of Art, Washington, DC,
Rosenwald Collection 1946.11.186

Mark Rothko (American, 1903–1970)
Untitled, 1946
Watercolor on paper, 38¼ × 25½″
Mr. and Mrs. Donald Blinken, New York (at
Heckscher Museum only)

Georges Rouault (French, 1871–1958)
Who Does Not Paint Himself a Face?, 1923   **86**
Plate 8 from the portfolio *Miserere*
Etching, aquatint, and roulette over heliogra-
vure, 22⁵⁄₁₆ × 16¹⁵⁄₁₆″
The Museum of Modern Art, New York. Gift of
the artist

Portrait of Charles Baudelaire, c. 1924–1927 **8**
Lithograph, 10⁷⁄₁₆ × 6½″
The Museum of Modern Art, New York. Gift of
Abby Aldrich Rockefeller

Beauty, 1926–1927   **41**
Plate XIV from *Les Fleurs du mal I,* 1966
Heliogravure, aquatint, burnisher, and dry-
point, 13⅞ × 10⅛″
Print Collection, The Miriam and Ira D. Wallach
Division of Art, Prints and Photographs, The
New York Public Library, Astor, Lenox and Til-
den Foundations

The Irreparable (*Satan III*), 1926–1927   **54**
Plate VIII from *Les Fleurs du mal I,* 1966
Etching, burnisher, drypoint, and heliogravure,
13⅞ × 10⅛″
Print Collection, The Miriam and Ira D. Wallach
Division of Art, Prints and Photographs, The
New York Public Library, Astor, Lenox and Til-
den Foundations

Woman Skeleton in Window, 1926–1927
Plate XI from *Les Fleurs du mal I,* 1966
Heliogravure, aquatint, roulette, burnisher, and
scraper, 14 × 10⅛″
Print Collection, The Miriam and Ira D. Wallach
Division of Art, Prints and Photographs, The
New York Public Library, Astor, Lenox and Til-
den Foundations

James Abbott McNeill Whistler (American, 1834–
1903)
The Old Rag Lady (*La vieille aux loques*), 1858
Etching, 8⅛ × 5¾″
S. P. Avery Collection, The Miriam and Ira D.
Wallach Division of Art, Prints and Photo-
graphs, The New York Public Library, Astor,
Lenox and Tilden Foundations

Street at Saverne, 1858
Etching, 8⅛ × 6³⁄₁₆″
S. P. Avery Collection, The Miriam and Ira D.
Wallach Division of Art, Prints and Photo-
graphs, The New York Public Library, Astor,
Lenox and Tilden Foundations

Rotherhithe, 1860
Etching, 10¹³⁄₁₆ × 7¹³⁄₁₆″
Harbor Gallery, New York (at Heckscher
Museum only)

List of Lenders

Axinn Library, Hofstra University
The Baltimore Museum of Art
Sarah Campbell Blaffer Foundation
Mr. and Mrs. Donald Blinken, New York
Blum Helman Gallery, New York
The Brooklyn Museum
The Carnegie Museum of Art
Sterling and Francine Clark Art Institute
Dedalus Foundation
Epstein Family Collection
The Fogg Art Museum, Harvard University Art Museums
Grunwald Center for the Graphic Arts, UCLA
The Armand Hammer Museum of Art and Cultural Center
Harbor Gallery, New York
Heckscher Museum
Hirshhorn Museum and Sculpture Garden, Smithsonian Institution
The Houghton Library, Harvard University
The Library of Congress
The Metropolitan Museum of Art
The Minneapolis Institute of Arts
Museum of Art, Rhode Island School of Design
Museum of Fine Arts, Boston
The Museum of Modern Art
National Gallery of Art, Washington, DC
National Gallery of Canada, Ottawa
The New York Public Library
The Phillips Collection
Pollock-Krasner House and Study Center
Private Collection
Rodin Museum, Philadelphia
Smith College Museum of Art
University Libraries, State University of New York at Stony Brook
Yale University Art Gallery
Richard Zeisler, New York
Jane Voorhees Zimmerli Art Museum, Rutgers, The State University of New Jersey

Index

114 Edouard Manet, *Cats' Rendezvous,* 1868

Designed by Martine Bruel

Set in Optima regular, medium and bold by Hamilton Phototype

Separations, printing and binding by New Interlitho S.p.A.